Historic Tales *of* BONITA

Historic Tales of BONITA

Mary E. Oswell

The History Press

Published by The History Press
Charleston, SC
www.historypress.com

Front cover, top: Flag raising on the top of San Miguel Mountain on July 4, 1890. *San Diego History Center*; *bottom*: Brookside Winery Tasting Room No. 7. *Bonita Museum & Cultural Center*. *Back cover, top*: The Bonita Store, January 1957. *San Diego History Center*; *inset*: Ella B. Allen, circa 1913. *Allen Mitchum Jr.*

First published 2018

Manufactured in the United States

ISBN 9781467139854

Library of Congress Control Number: 2018942432

I dedicate this book to everyone who ever lived in Bonita or Sunnyside *or the Sweetwater Valley. Bonita is my hometown, and whether it has readily discernable boundaries or not, it is clear that Bonita is a state of mind, and though one may leave, Bonita stays in your heart forever.*

CONTENTS

ACKNOWLEDGEMENTS

The completion of this work would not have been possible without the assistance of a variety of institutions. I would like to express my gratitude to the archivists and historians at the Smithsonian National Air and Space Museum, Hyde County Historical and Genealogical Society, the California Genealogical Society and Library, the Japanese-American Historical Society of San Diego, the San Diego Air & Space Museum Library and Archives, the National City Public Library Local History Room, the Chula Vista Public Library, the Special Collections of the San Diego Public Library and the San Diego History Center Research Library. I would also like to thank the following individuals who shared their stories and photographs with me: Bob and Patty Basile, Herb Aarlie, Virginia Crumrine, Maryanne Savary, Mike Campbell, Glenn and Jo Morrison, Melodi Morrison, and Pamela Lennen of the Salvation Army.

Thanks to Susan Schnare, who was always willing to lend me a hand and share her accumulated wisdom and knowledge about Robert Morris Copeland and his life and landscape gardening career with me.

Two members of the Allen family went above and beyond: Rick Sherman, whose family history (*The Ancestry of Samuel Sterling Sherman and Mary Ware Allen*) was the foundation for my journey into of the lives of Russell and Ella Allen, and Beau Mitchum, who supplied photographs and audio clips of family history and was continually supportive of my efforts.

The Bonita Museum & Cultural Center is where all of my digging started when I walked in the door one day fifteen years ago and asked if there was something I could help them with. Thanks to the museum's many volunteers over the years and Director Julie Gay, who opened up the museum's archives to me whenever I needed it and offered her assistance at every turn.

Finally, my husband, Stan, endured the many hours I worked on the book and listened to many more hours of my talking about Bonita. Your patience and kindness throughout this process was notable. My journey wouldn't be the same without you.

INTRODUCTION

In the course of researching local history, it is not uncommon to come across fascinating stories that are not part of your primary research goal. You encounter interesting people whose stories have never been told yet may be fundamental to the community's history. There were businesses that were the heart and soul of a neighborhood that have long been forgotten. There are entire districts that were created and disappeared overnight that are now just a footnote in a larger story.

Sometimes it's possible to fit these stories into a larger narrative, but other times you're just left with a fascinating story and nowhere to use it. The genesis of this book is these orphan stories that have not seen the light of day because I could never fit them into the larger narrative of my work at the Bonita Museum and Cultural Center. Some of these stories unfold over decades, and others came and went in the blink of an eye. But all of them have a place in the larger story of the small community that is Bonita and its place in San Diego County. Though many just see Bonita as a pretty name someone slapped on a housing development, that's not the reality. Bonita was here before the developer's bulldozers came to change the landscape.

So, the first question about Bonita usually is, "Why is it called Bonita?" Bonita does mean "pretty" in Spanish, though it is usually used as a descriptor, so a town might be called like Bonita Springs or Bonita Falls. This Bonita is just Bonita. And so, you have to go way back to the era of Frank Kimball to get your answer.

When Frank and his brothers purchased El Rancho de la Nación in 1868, they had a lot of dreams for the future but not a lot of ways to actually make money. Over the years, the Kimballs made many attempts to make the land profitable while they were waiting for the railroad to arrive and the dam to be finished. Frank Kimball grew citrus and olives and manufactured them into products; he also created a brickyard and built a set of row houses for the railroad workers. By 1872, the Kimballs were raising sheep in the valley, primarily for wool. The Sweetwater Valley was not a bad place to raise sheep, but it didn't have a constant source of water, as the river was prone to drying up in the summer. In 1873, in addition to building a corral and a small shed, Frank built an earth dam across an area that filled with water when the river was high. The small lake that accumulated allowed him to have a source of water for the sheep in the drier months. By 1877, he had built a wooden culvert to accomplish this. In his extensive diaries, which are held at the National City Public Library, he begins by referring to this as his "little lake," but eventually, he starts to call it "Laguna Bonita." It was located to the west of the present-day Willow Street Bridge. By 1882, he had given up raising sheep, though he continued to maintain the culvert for the water it stored.

In 1883, Henry Cooper purchased acreage from Frank Kimball to start a citrus ranch. The property was located to the east of the lake, on the south side of the river. Cooper referred to his property as Bonita Ranch, likely because of its proximity to the lake.

Cooper, like just about everybody else in Southern California in the 1880s, was swept up in the land boom, and with his law background, knew how to go forward with creating a town. In 1887, he created a subdivision map, and he called it "The Town of Bonita." It was a heady time, and the map is somewhat unrealistic in its portrayal of what might eventually be a town. At almost the same time, in June 1887, the National City and Otay Railroad began operations in the valley. The route left National City and came east up the valley with stops at Lynwood Grove, Bonita, Bonnie Brae and the Sweetwater Dam, ending at La Presa. Those early stops may have had only wooden signs to designate them, but they reinforced the place names to passengers. Laguna Bonita was eventually set aside by Kimball in 1887 as part of the Lynwood Grove picnic area.

When the Sweetwater Fruit Company built a mercantile in 1892, it named the business the Bonita Store, and the post office was established in Bonita in 1898. By that time, the name was firmly connected to the land, and that's how Bonita got its name.

1
THE BOSTON TO BONITA CONNECTION

The first permanent residents in the Sweetwater Valley were certainly gentleman farmers. They brought capital from a variety of other businesses, and though they successfully produced and sold their citrus, they did not approach citrus growing as a business. The next wave of men and women, however, elevated the production of citrus to a business and helped create the district known as Bonita. To understand how and why a group of Bostonians became the founders of Bonita's citrus business, you have to understand the development of the railroad in Kansas. Yes, Kansas. It may seem a bit out of the way, but in reality, it is a direct line to the development of the Sweetwater Valley, Bonita and Sunnyside.

In the mid-1800s the most important factor for business success in America was the ability to move goods and people. And in general, that was done most effectively with the railroad. The rail system independently grew all across the nation—from one town to another—and then connected those short sections all across the nation.

The man who created the Atchison Topeka and Santa Fe (ATSF) Railroad, Cyrus K. Holliday, envisioned a railroad that would stretch from Kansas all the way to the Pacific Ocean. He began, however, with a small line running from Topeka to Carbondale (where a large coal mine was located). In order to get even a short line in operation, Holliday had to have land on which to build his railroad and money to cover the building costs. The U.S. government gave him a land grant, and he was able to build many miles of tracks. But by September 1868, the money raised from the initial stock offering had run out, and the men who had the most invested in the company took over control. It was through these men that the firm of Kidder Peabody became involved in the ATSF.

Kidder Peabody was a U.S. securities firm whose operations included investment banking and stock buying and trading. The investors behind the ATSF Railroad signed a contract with Kidder Peabody to sell the railroad's securities. Using the land grants awarded by the U.S. government and with funds raised by bonds from counties along the way, the railroad was able to make progress across Kansas. Eventually, the railroad and its investors sold nearly three million acres of land in Kansas and made a profit of $7 million (over $100 million in today's dollars). Selling land to family farmers rather than speculators, the investors ensured that their railroad would continue to have plenty of business moving people and products. Though the railroad's fortunes ebbed and flowed, it continued toward its ultimate goal of the Pacific Ocean.

In 1868, Frank Kimball and his brother Warren purchased the Rancho de La Nación, a rancho that covered present-day National City, Bonita and Chula Vista. In order to fulfill his dreams for National City, Frank knew that he needed a railroad connection. His first attempt to bring a railroad to National City, in 1869, never advanced beyond the paper stage, and his later attempts also failed. By the mid-1870s, the public had soured on giving land to the railroads, and the ATSF was looking for other ways to finish its line to the Pacific.

With large tracks of land and some money from the local city governments, Frank Kimball was able to convince Kidder Peabody and the investors of the ATSF to choose San Diego (more specifically National City) as the terminus of their line. On July 10, 1880, a contract was signed to connect San Diego with the Santa Fe line, creating the California Southern Railroad. California Southern received 17,356 acres of land (the remainder of the Rancho de la Nación land in 1880), two miles of harbor front property, plots of land for a depot and terminal space and over $25,000 in cash.

This land deal spurred creation of the San Diego Land and Town Company, a joint interest of the Kimball brothers and the California Southern (including Kidder Peabody) and gave the Land and Town Company five years of exclusive rights to sell the ten thousand acres granted to the new railroad. In 1886, to ensure the success of the venture, the Land and Town Company brought in William Green Dickinson. Dickinson had joined the Arkansas Valley Land and Town Company, associated with the Atchison in Kansas, in 1874. It is said that he laid out and managed one hundred towns along railroad lines of Kansas during his time. Through the Land and Town Company, Dickinson was responsible for the plotting and sale of the land in Chula Vista, and he also oversaw the completion of the Sweetwater Dam and the National City and Otay Railroad. After Dickinson's death in 1891, his son-in-law John E. Boal took over as the manager of the Land and Town Company.

Kidder Peabody and the Boston investors in the railroad must have been looking forward to prosperous days of land sales in San Diego, but this was not to be. Though the California Southern was built and did connect San Diego and the Sweetwater Valley (through the National City and Otay Railroad completed in 1887) to the rest of the United States, the land boom was about to come to an end. In January and February 1884, the loss of thirty miles of rails to flooding in Temecula Canyon forced California Southern near to bankruptcy. Quick work by the investors saved the California Southern line from bankruptcy, but they were bought out by the Santa Fe, fulfilling Holliday's dream of a railroad to the Pacific. The expense of sailing cargo ships from San Diego to San Francisco was high, and shipments from Kansas to San Diego did not materialize. The ATSF Railroad quietly negotiated with Southern Pacific to use its lines into Los Angeles. In 1885, the main rail yard, which had been located in National City, was moved to San Bernardino, and in 1888, a new line south from Los Angeles bypassed Temecula Canyon. Frank Kimball's dream of being the western terminus of a railroad was essentially dead. San Diego would forevermore be a spur line. However, the railroad boom had increased the local population and property values.

When the land boom went bust, the Boston investors and the railroad still owned thousands of acres of land, much of it in the Sweetwater Valley. When the Land and Town Company started to plant citrus trees on lots as an inducement to sell acreage, a new company formed to buy land with the express purpose of growing citrus. In the *San Diego Union* of June 21, 1890, it was reported that the "articles of incorporation of the Sweetwater Fruit Company were filed Thursday," and it listed Robert Winsor, R.C. Allen, Richard H. Weld, Herbert Dabney and F.E. Prendergast as the first directors.

Family connections, lifelong friendships and Harvard were at the core of the Sweetwater Fruit Company. But the connections started with Robert Winsor. After graduating from Harvard in 1880, Robert Winsor went to work as a clerk at Kidder Peabody. By 1890, he was only four years away from being named a partner in the firm, fourteen years from clerk to partner

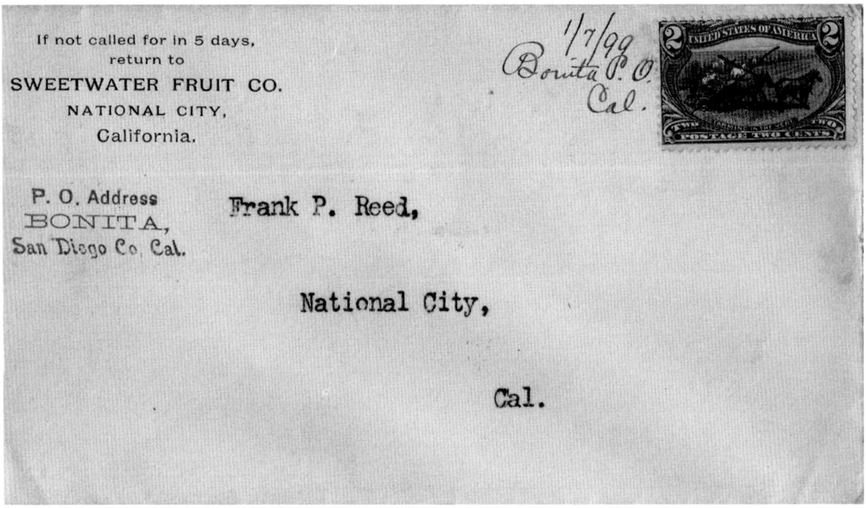

A Sweetwater Fruit Company envelope with a Bonita Post Office cancellation from 1899. *Author's collection.*

being quite a meteoric rise. He could see the success of the Land and Town Company's agricultural ventures, though its efforts were secondary to the desire to sell land. Winsor brought together his firm and the extensive familial connections he had from Boston to fill out the first slate of officers and investors for the new company.

Smack dab in the center of this new operation was Russell C. Allen. Allen was a transplant from Boston to California who had some previous experience in running a successful fruit growing operation. After graduating from Harvard, Allen spent a year reading law, but he had lost the sight in his eye as the result of a childhood baseball accident, and the strain of so much reading made him reconsider his career path. He decided to change to a "outdoor life" and began to look for possibilities at every turn. In early 1883, Allen embarked on a trip to California, leaving Boston and arriving on the east coast of Panama before traveling up the west coast of Central America and arriving in San Diego in November 1882. In 1883, he purchased a property in Dehesa on the eastern end of the Sweetwater Valley, 280 acres, and planted a grape vineyard and an olive orchard. Though he did not come from a farming background, he took to that life quite well and, in the ensuing years, succeeded. In addition to running the ranch, Allen also was head of the El Cajon Packing Company.

Allen's connections to Robert Winsor were strong: both were members of the class of 1880 at Harvard, and they were also second cousins, both great-grandsons of Reverend Henry Ware, an influential Unitarian theologian. Allen's wife, Ella, was a friend of Winsor's and attended school with him as a child. Allen and Winsor had traveled together in April 1890, when they visited Washington, D.C., and Guadalajara, only two months before the announcement of the incorporation of the company.

Richard Harding Weld also attended Harvard (graduating in 1856) and was Robert Winsor's first cousin by marriage through Laura Townsend Winsor. He was a merchandise broker, specializing in hemp and jute, and worked for most of his career at the firm his father founded, Aaron D. Weld & Sons. He never set up a residence in the valley, but he did visit, often staying with Robert Winsor. He was the only member of the new venture who had a position of authority at the San Diego Land and Town Company, having been a director and vice president. (There is evidence of other members of San Diego Land and Town having investment in the Sweetwater Fruit Company, but they were negligible investors.) After

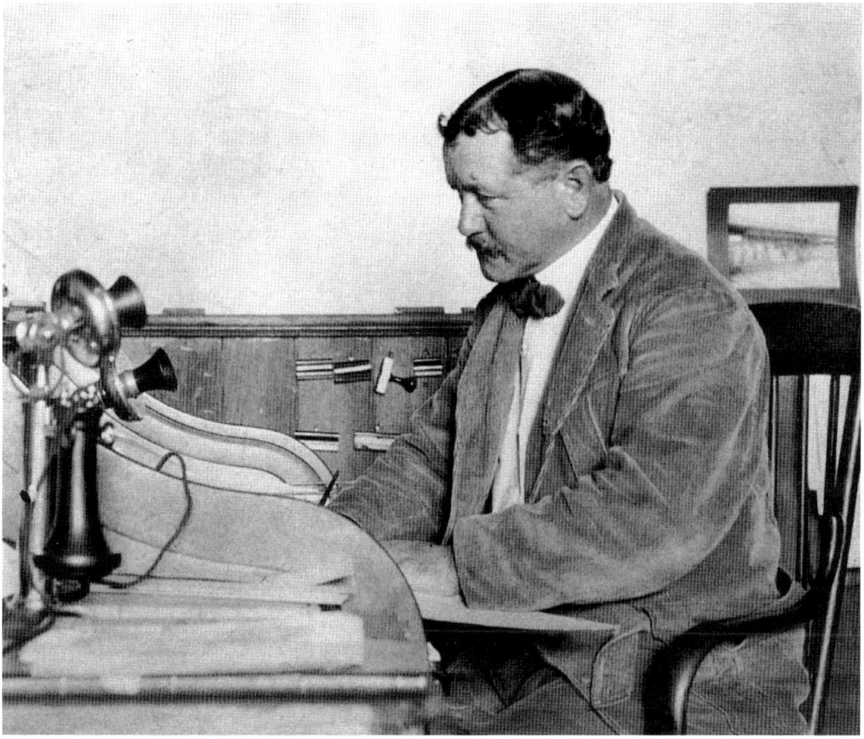

Russell C. Allen working at his desk in the Sweetwater Fruit Company offices, 1914.
California Genealogical Society, Manuscript Collection.

Weld died in 1908, his son Richard Harding Weld Jr., who worked with his father at the family firm, took over as president of the Sweetwater Fruit Company.

Herbert Dabney was from a prominent wealthy Boston family who had since the early 1800s been merchants in the Azores, living on the island of Fayal. His father, grandfather and great-grandfather had been U.S. consuls to the Azores, and Herbert was born there in 1853. He attended MIT and returned to Fayal to work in the family business until 1890. At the time of the incorporation of the Sweetwater Fruit Company, Herbert had been a partner to Russell Allen in the El Cajon Packing Company, which specialized in packing and distributing raisins. Herbert moved to California in 1890 and was most well known in San Diego County for managing the San Diego, Pacific Beach and La Jolla Railway (a commuter line that traveled north out of downtown San Diego). He lived in Coronado for many years but returned to Boston in 1902 after leaving the railway and lived there until his death in 1920.

Francis Ensor Prendergast was a civil engineer, educated at the University of Dublin, who came to the United States in 1868 to work on the Transcontinental Railroad. He worked for a variety of railways on both sides of the ocean for over twenty-five years, ending up in Sault Ste. Marie as the resident engineer for the St. Mary's Falls Water Power Company when the company ran out of funds for its project in 1889. At that time, Prendergast accepted a position as the horticultural superintendent for the San Diego Land and Town Company, selecting plants, configuring the land and overseeing the care of the citrus groves. As Prendergast lacked a Boston connection, his work for the Land and Town Company must have brought him to the attention of the founders of the Sweetwater Fruit Company, including R.H. Weld. Being one of the rare folks for whom San Diego's climate was not ideal, for health reasons Prendergast moved to Redlands, California, in 1893, where he continued to oversee citrus groves until his death in 1897.

Winsor brought together funds and expertise from himself, Weld, Allen, Dabney and Prendergast to originate this new company. The company offered stock valued at $100,000; over $35,000 had been sold as of incorporation. The company purchased the ranch of Henry Cooper, which included 115 acres, 35 of which were under cultivation. Additional parcels were purchased, mostly from the San Diego Land and Town Company, to create a ranch of over 200 acres. Initial efforts on the ranch included planting 40 acres of walnuts near the riverbed, but those trees were not

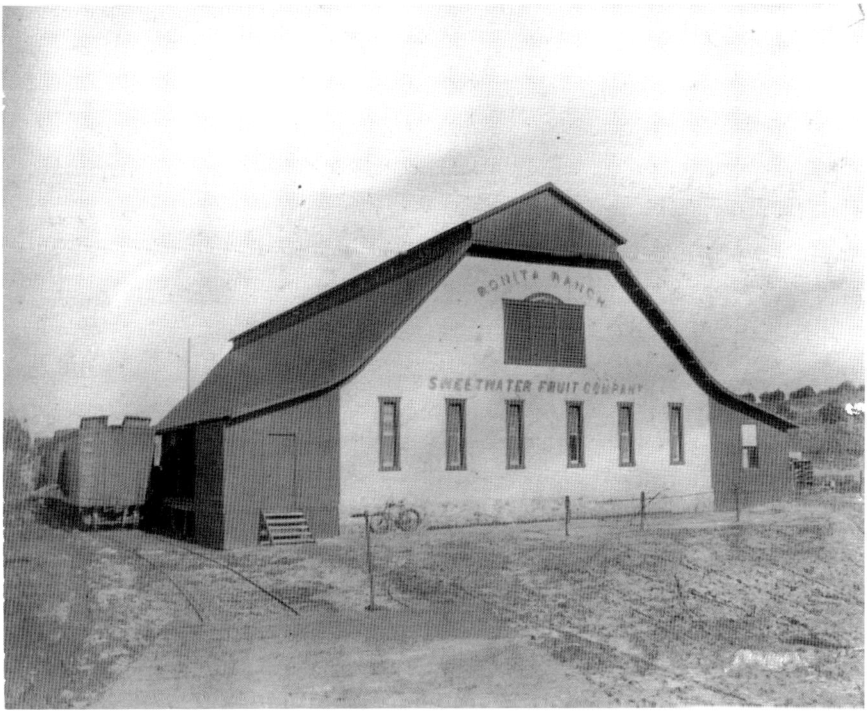

This photo from the late 1890s shows the National City & Otay Railroad siding next to the Sweetwater Fruit Company packing house. *Bonita Museum & Cultural Center.*

successful and the orchard was not replanted after flooding occurred in 1895. The company did grow guavas for many years, having as many as two thousand bushes producing nearly five tons. The fruit was made into jelly on the Bonita property and sent east for sale.

Late in 1890, the Sweetwater Fruit Company began construction of a barn. By 1894, it had built an adobe packing house to support its operation and added a wooden storage facility around 1900. No one is quite sure why the owners choose adobe, as adobe was not widely used in San Diego at that time. However, the house that R.C. Allen built in Dehesa was made of adobe, and he must have learned to appreciate its insulating properties during the warm summer months. In 1891, Sweetwater Fruit Company built the Bonita Store, a small clapboard structure with a residence on the back for the proprietor. In 1898, Bonita got its own post office, located in the store. In its first ten years in operation, the Sweetwater Fruit Company produced lemons and oranges in Bonita and olives in Dehesa to great success, and Russell Allen became much in demand to speak and write about his expertise in cultivation.

The Sweetwater Fruit Company reorganized in 1906 as a California company, and many of the eastern investors did not return, though Robert Winsor did. The operation of the Sweetwater Fruit Company also brought workers to the valley, and behind the packing shed, the company built several small houses, which it rented to employees, as well as other garage and shed buildings. These workers included immigrants, and early on, the company employed Chinese labor. However, the number of Chinese workers dwindled in the years after the Chinese Exclusion Act of 1882. Economic conditions in Japan at the turn of the nineteenth century were such that opportunities were scarce. The presence of larger numbers of Japanese workers in the early 1900s can be seen in the emergence of Japanese-run labor camps in the South Bay. The Shimokawa Camp was established in Bonita in 1908, using a bunkhouse that was previously built on the fruit ranch's property to house workers. Using a "boss" (a Japanese immigrant who had lived in the United States long enough to understand the language and U.S. labor practices) as an intermediary between the worker and employer, this system gave employment, housing and meals to the Japanese immigrants and a steady stream of reliable workers to the orchard owners. Many of the Japanese workers would eventually buy their own land and become farmers in their own right, especially in the celery industry in Chula Vista as the camp system started to fade in the early 1920s. In addition, smaller but significant numbers of workers from Mexico were employed by the company.

Picking lemons involved using ladders to reach the fruit, the stem of which was cut from the branch. Those stems were then cut off so as to not bruise the fruit during preparation. Fruit was then washed in a soapy solution, dried on runners, graded and sorted, with the best fruit being boxed and sent to cure. Fruit that could not be sold in markets was sent for processing into lemon juice and citric acid, both of which were valuable commodities. Built in 1898, the California Citrus Products Company processing plant made citric acid and oil of lemon and was located in National City until 1954. The company also bought unsellable fruit from lemon trees growing in the South Bay. In addition to pickers, the Sweetwater Fruit Company employed pruners, sprayers and fumigators in the orchards as well as foremen for each crew and a manager for the orchards. In the packing house, workers were needed to supervise the washing and grading of fruit and to assemble crates, as well as to pack

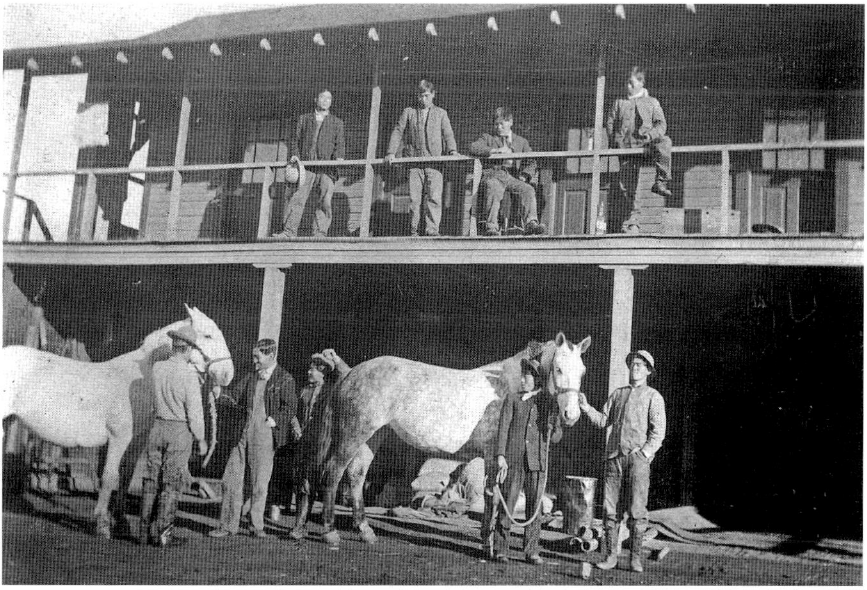

Japanese workers in Sunday clothes at the Sweetwater Fruit Company's bunkhouse. *Japanese American Historical Society of San Diego.*

crates for storage or into railroad cars (later trucks) for transportation. Close to half of the workers in packing houses in California were women, something that is borne out in census records for Bonita as well.

After many years of traveling to Bonita to oversee his investments, in 1913, Robert Winsor built a house on the north rim of the valley. It was designed by Frank Mead and Richard Requa. Mead had worked for Hebbard and Gill's firm before they broke up and had partnered with Gill in 1907. In 1912, Requa, who had worked for Gill as a project superintendent, began a partnership with Mead. In the house they designed for Robert Winsor, they created a structure to harmonize with the surroundings. The design included a central open courtyard, a roof loggia and a pergola, all of which highlight the views of the surrounding valley. In addition, Kate Sessions designed the landscaping for the home, including a rose garden.

In addition to the investors that Russell Allen and Robert Winsor brought to Bonita, they also brought other family members. One of the earliest doctors to take up residence in the valley was Franklin Asaph Dunbar. Dunbar was a first cousin of Ella B. Copeland, Russell's wife, and the two had spent many days together as children. A member of the class of 1878

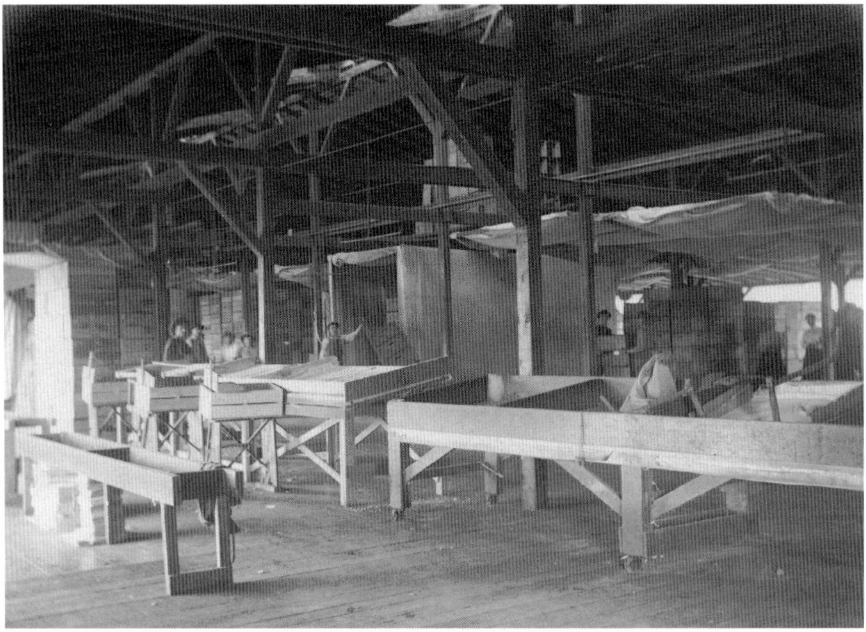

The interior of the packing house where workers are stacking crates to be stored between canvas partitions. *Allen Mitchum Jr.*

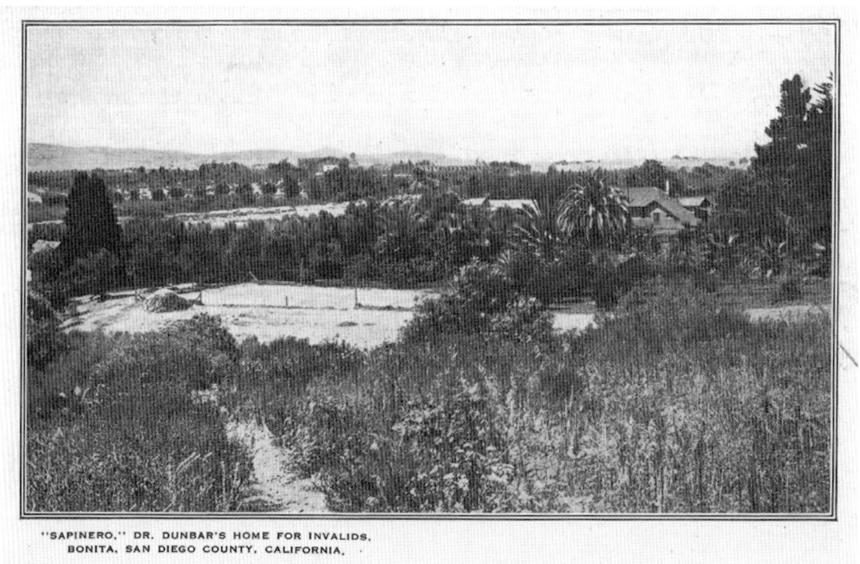

A postcard image of Dr. Dunbar's home and sanitarium, which was located near where Rohr Manor stands today. *Author's collection.*

at Harvard, after receiving his medical degree in 1883, Dunbar was the inspector of milk and vinegar for the city of Cambridge for fifteen years. It was a well-paid position ($900 a year), though it took only an hour of his day, five days a week. He left this job to come west in 1901 and bought the home and property of B.F. Wells, who had remodeled the existing adobe built by Don Juan Forster on the edge of the river bottom into a new structure. In addition to ministering to the local residents, Dr. Dunbar hosted invalids in need of recuperation at this home, and his sanitarium was advertised in many East Coast publications. He was the local doctor until his death in 1932.

Though the flood of 1916 did cause extensive damage in the valley, the freeze of 1913 was more destructive to the lemon operations. In 1912, the Sweetwater Fruit Company planted a new grove on the land where Valley Vista Elementary now stands and the freeze of 1913 required that entire orchard be replanted in addition to the damage the freeze did to existing trees. Prior to the 1913 freeze, most lemons grown in the valley were Lisbon or Villafranca varieties, which yielded their biggest crops in late winter. This necessitated storage of the bulk of the crop for several months until summer, when the greatest demand for lemons existed. In the wake of the death of trees in 1913, most trees were replaced by Eureka lemons, which produce heavily in the summer and didn't need to be stored for as long.

The 1916 flood did wash away the sides of the packing house, which were quickly replaced by wood. (In the ensuing years, the walls were painted red, which is how the packing house became known as the Red Barn.) The removal of the debris washed into the valley took longer, but the lemon orchards, which were built on the bluffs overlooking the river, were largely undamaged. The owners of the National City and Otay Railroad determined that replacing the line up the valley was not cost effective, and they pulled up whatever rails could be salvaged before leaving for good. A new loading dock was built on the west side of the barn for loading trucks, which were able to pick up the slack delivering lemons to market. Passenger travel in and out of the valley was harder to replace, as roads that served the area were not paved until late in the 1920s.

Fruit sales continued to do well into the 1920s. Floods in 1927 again damaged the packing house, and the Sweetwater Fruit Company moved its packing operation to National City near the railroad line. Also in 1927, the death of Russell Allen forced the company to reorganize, with Russell's son Richard taking over management of the operation. (Richard had been working with his father since he returned from college in 1915.) The original wooden Bonita Store building was cramped and old, and the company replaced it with a larger stucco building on the south side of the road. The new establishment included gas pumps, a necessity in a world where car travel had taken over. The company also was part of a group that started the Sweetwater Cooperative Citrus Association in 1929, which helped all the growers in the valley market their fruit.

In 1931, the company was reorganized by the Allens, Boals and Campbells as the Sweetwater Fruit Company Inc., increasing the capitol stock to $250,000, keeping ownership of the company within the family. The Depression years were lean ones, but the company continued to thrive. A total of 724 rail cars of lemons were sent from the South Bay in 1934, returning $2.38 of profit on each box. (In 1932, there were 140,000 lemon trees growing in the South Bay, that number being nearly 5 percent of all bearing lemon trees in the United States.) The years during World War II were difficult, as field workers were hard to find. The old packing house was used to house men who came from Mexico as part of the Bracero Program to work in the orchards, as able-bodied U.S. citizens were involved in the war effort and the Japanese Americans had been sent to internment camps.

The postwar years brought an increase in cost and decrease in availability of water and a rise in the value of land for houses, all issues that made for troubled times in the citrus industry. In 1946, the company decided to close its National City packing house and arrange for the Chula Vista Fruit Growers Exchange to pack its fruit. At the same time, the increased population in the valley desired more commercial enterprises to meet their needs without having to drive to Chula Vista. The company did work to bring new business to the valley, opening La Tienda, a combination hardware/sundries store and lunch counter that also included a small office for the company. The company also built a separate gas station across the road from the Bonita Store. The businesses and building were owned and operated by the Sweetwater Fruit Company.

In the years after World War II, land in the Sweetwater Valley was becoming more valuable as residential property than as orchards and agricultural fields. The year 1947 was the last one in which the valley's landowners considered lemons to be a prime source of their income. In 1948, Richard M. Allen, who had run the Sweetwater Fruit Company since his father's death, sold off the first piece of the original land that his father had acquired in 1890, a subdivision of twelve one-acre lots. As time went on, the quality and cost of water to irrigate fruit trees became a snowballing issue for the Sweetwater Fruit Company, an added pressure to the increasing population and property values. Russell Allen's children and the other members of the company could see that the valley was changing from an agricultural district to a bedroom community. The increase in population in the valley pushed the formation of a volunteer fire department, whose first firefighting equipment was a sprayer truck donated by the company and housed near the packing house.

It was in the years after World War II that the packing house began being referred to as the Old Red Barn. Prior to that, it was usually referred to as the packing house or maybe the old packing house in Bonita. And we're not sure how far back it was painted red, unfortunately, though we know the pine paneling was first added after the 1916 flood. After the Sweetwater Fruit Company stopped using the structure for packing and storing citrus, it offered it out to a variety of uses, including Farm Bureau meetings and rabies vaccination clinics. During the time the barn was used for stabling horses and mules, a horse ring was built on the east side of the barn, and local teenagers used it to give horse riding lessons. The Upper Sweetwater Valley Volunteer Fire Protection District hosted two horse shows at the barn to raise funds for the department. In 1951, the Bonita-Sunnyside Fire Protection District opened the first firehouse on land donated by the Sweetwater Fruit Company. Bonita's 4-H Club used the barn for Field Day events and livestock judging to prepare for the local county fair from 1949 to 1960. Over the years, several businesses rented space in the barn, including a feed store, a blacksmith and an antiques store. In addition to its working life, the Old Red Barn has been the subject of countless works of art, most prominently by Gladys Day, a local artist.

In 1957, the company had an appraisal of its holdings completed, which included the Bonita Store, the La Tienda Fountain Lunch, a service station, the former packing house, five employee cottages, four small garage units, five other small buildings, as well as over 250 acres of orchards and unimproved land. The value of its holdings was placed just under $1 million, about $25 million in 2018 dollars. After long family discussions, in June 1957, the Sweetwater Fruit Company was dissolved, with unsold land placed into a trust for continued sale. In addition to the cost of water and the increasing value of the land, Richard Allen placed a portion of the blame on lower citrus sales on people drinking less cooling lemonade because of air conditioning. Progress had brought an end to the Sweetwater Fruit Company after nearly sixty years. In March 1960, the Old Red Barn, built in 1894, was dismantled

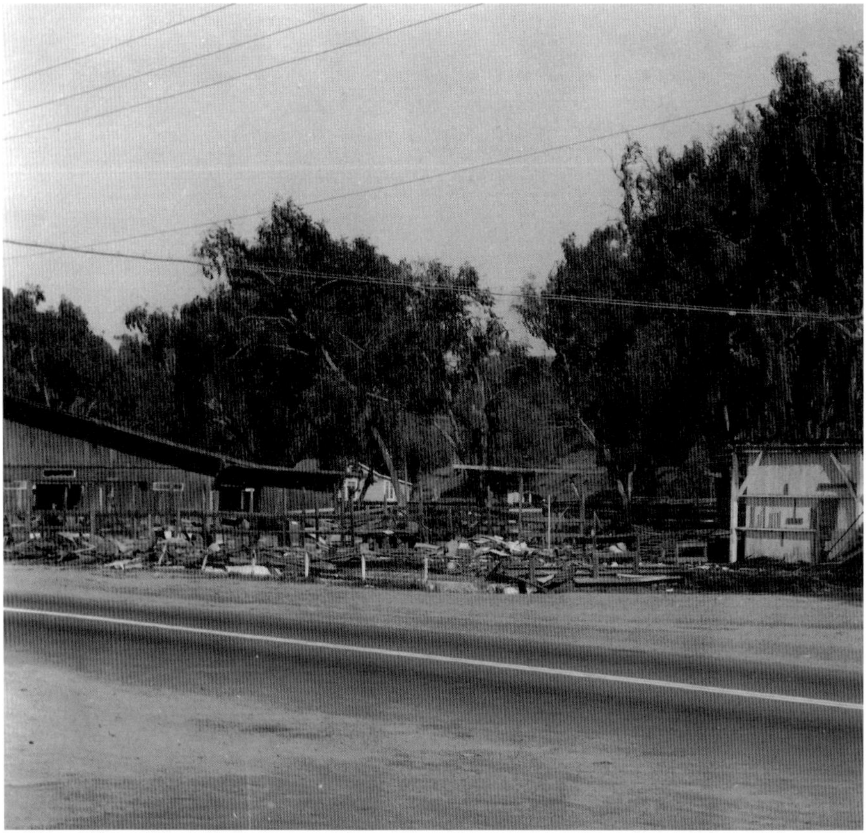

In March 1960, the Old Red Barn was torn down to make room for a larger shopping district in Bonita. *Bonita Museum & Cultural Center.*

to make room for a shopping center. The stucco Bonita Store building and the brick building at 4020 Bonita Road are the only two structures that remain of those built for the Sweetwater Fruit Company. It was a sad day when the iconic barn came down, but the community that surrounded it was a testament to the founders of the Sweetwater Fruit Company and their vision for what the valley could become.

2

MISSING SAN MIGUEL

Where Was It and Why Is It Gone?

It would be difficult to imagine that a mountain that's over 2,500 feet high, sitting just a few miles from San Diego Bay, could be considered missing. It's a looming presence anywhere in the South Bay. However, considering how many failed endeavors and lost causes might have been built on and around the mountain, it's also hard to admit that San Miguel Mountain's chronicle isn't just a tiny bit misplaced.

It is sure that the Kumeyaay who lived at the base of this mountain had a name for this geological feature, but unfortunately, that name is gone. There are, in fact, maps showing Native American trails that go back to before the time the mountain was named by Europeans. We also don't know for sure who named it San Miguel Mountain or Mount San Miguel or just Mount Miguel, but Sierra de San Miguel is the way it is noted on the 1843 hand-drawn map that was used to patent El Rancho de la Nación. San Miguel, or Saint Michael, was a very popular name for things during the Spanish Californian period. When he sailed into the bay in 1542, Juan Rodríguez Cabrillo named the location San Miguel because his first full day on location was the feast of San Miguel. When Sebastián Vizcaíno sailed into the bay in 1602, it was the feast day of San Diego de Álcala, and that was the name that stuck. Either way, San Miguel Mountain is firmly rooted in the history of the region.

In 1873, Frank Kimball sold a large portion of San Miguel Mountain and its surrounding area to George Copeland. Copeland and his wife built a farmhouse, windmill and vineyard not far from the shore of the Sweetwater

Reservoir. Things remained quiet at the base of San Miguel Mountain until the land boom of the late 1880s.

The Pacific Coast Land Bureau, a branch of a larger California real estate auction house, had a history of subdividing and selling large parcels of property in Tulare and Kern Counties and even on the island of Coronado. Sometimes it owned the land, and occasionally, it partnered with the owners. Late in the spring of 1887, the Pacific Coast Land Bureau was approached by Copeland, who owned over 350 acres along the southern edge of the Sweetwater Reservoir, about subdividing and selling lots. It was quite a heady time in the land boom in 1887, and as the National City and Otay Railroad had recently announced its intention to continue the line to nearby in La Presa, it seemed an opportune time to sell.

The Pacific Coast Land Bureau had been authorized to survey and subdivide the acreage, which it called San Miguel City, and made a preliminary map. It appears that on the afternoon of Sunday, July 10, the owners of the land brought some friends to the Land Bureau office in San Diego to look at the preliminary map and choose some choice lots for themselves ahead of the opening of the sale to the general public. Overseeing the sales was the local manager for Pacific Coast Land Bureau, R.J. Pennell. Other people in the office witnessed these transactions and were swept up in the moment and put down payments on the $50 lots for a subdivision in a place they had likely never seen. Word of mouth drove those sales to continue until ten o'clock at night, when Pennell finally decided he had to close up shop. The next day, visits to the office continued at a brisk pace, and the newspaper reported that three hundred lots had been sold at the end of that day, making over $130,000 in sales. One newspaper called it "the Real Estate Craze."

Because of the number of sales, a few days later, the Pacific Coast Land Bureau planned an excursion from its offices for the buyers to go and visit the land they had purchased. On July 17, organizers borrowed buggies and wagons from just about everywhere they could find, charged one dollar for the round trip, and took quite a number of people out to see the location. The festivities even included a brass band. But when the vehicles returned to downtown, there were buyers who felt that they wanted a refund, and a dissatisfied group of purchasers planned to hire a lawyer to see if the title was clouded so they could get out of the deal.

Once the newspapers got hold of the story, accusations flew in all directions—to the Pacific Coast Land Bureau, its owners, its representatives and the owners of the land. The managers in charge of the Pacific Coast Land Bureau, Wendell Easton and G.W. Frink, jumped on the train from

Los Angeles to visit San Diego and sort out the issues. They announced that the title on the land, which had not yet been published, was just fine, and that everyone involved should go ahead with their purchases, as there was no cloud on ownership. They also expressed a concern that people had purchased lots with the express idea of reselling them at an increased value, an idea they discouraged and found to be troublesome. One newspaper editorial called the lots "utterly worthless and the location is as odious as the lots are valueless." Another called San Miguel "an obscure place." It appeared that viewing the locale of their purchases gave a lot of folks buyer's remorse. Easton and Frink, however, decided to quietly return money to those who felt swindled—to preserve their reputations, if for no other reason. By late summer, the outrage had subsided.

By late 1888, it was clear that the boom had faded, and no city was going to flourish at San Miguel. Some people did build homes in the area, and in 1888, there were enough local residents to create a San Miguel School District. The first classes were held in a private home, but a school was built near today's Proctor Valley Road and Hunte Parkway. The San Miguel School District remained active for quite a few years, finally lapsing in 1918. In 1889, a large portion of the San Miguel City site was sold to J.W. Reed, who intended to plant citrus.

In addition to its desirability as a backdrop for homes, San Miguel Mountain had been seen since the 1880s as an appropriate location for a large telescope. Astronomy achieved a measure of public success in this time, with a large number of professors giving regular lectures for the general public. Richard A. Proctor was a professor of astronomy from England who became a well-known popular author and speaker. A series of poor financial decisions left him without a regular salary, and he had taken to writing popularized astronomy books to get by. He traveled extensively and gave lectures in the United States as early as 1874. Proctor's personal life was slightly complicated; he and his ill wife had decamped to Australia from England in 1880 for her health, at which time they met another couple, Robert and Sallie Crawley. Both Proctor's wife and Crawley's husband died later that year, and the remaining spouses' friendship bloomed into romance. They were married in May 1881 in Missouri (where the new Mrs. Proctor had previously lived) and took up residence there in 1884.

In 1886, the University of Southern California planned to open a campus in San Diego to be called the San Diego College of Arts and Sciences. The school had discussions with Richard Proctor about becoming astronomy professor on its new campus, and it is believed he made visits to Southern California as part of those discussions, although we do not know if he visited San Diego. Richard and Sallie relocated to Florida in 1887, and in September 1888, Richard headed to New York to depart on a European lecture tour. He arrived in New York ill, and the local doctors were concerned that he had yellow fever and sent him to isolation. He died and was buried in an obscure corner of a Brooklyn cemetery. (It was later determined that he had suffered from malaria, making moving him to isolation a contributing factor in his death.) At the time of Richard's untimely death in September 1888, the university had broken ground on a campus in University Heights, roughly at Park and University Boulevards. However, the end of the land boom forced USC to stop the project roughly at the same time that Richard died.

Richard's grieving widow, after finalizing his estates in England and the United States, found herself without sufficient funds to live on. She had assisted her husband with his observations and the preparations of his books and had become somewhat proficient in the subject of astronomy, so in 1889, she began to deliver his lectures and slide shows herself. She also wished to move forward with a project to honor Richard, and she believed building a large land-based telescope would be an appropriate monument. At that time, most telescopes were located on the East Coast—surrounded by cities—and light pollution was becoming an issue for their continued operation. In fact, as early as 1885, there had been people calling for the addition of an observatory to the top of San Miguel Mountain.

Enter Alfred Isham, a New York businessman who had moved to San Diego in 1885. He was involved in several local business endeavors with other prominent local men, such as H.L. Story and Frank Kimball. Possibly influenced by lectures that Sallie had given in San Diego, Alfred Isham and Story in March 1890 bought 160 acres atop San Miguel from Frank Reed, who had purchased it in 1888. They announced that they intended to build a "pleasure park," including an observatory, a hotel grander than the Hotel Del Coronado and a gondola ride up the mountain.

Isham, who could charm the bark off a tree, convinced the widow Proctor to participate in an event on the top of the mountain so they could show the entire city how important and special the observatory could be. They planned this event to coincide with the Fourth of July and to include a fireworks display attempting to duplicate the eruption of Vesuvius. (Isham was never content with anything less than over the top.) Mrs. Proctor had previously made visits to the Lick Observatory in May 1890 and consulted with her colleagues about the suitability of building an observatory.

The party, consisting of twelve men and eight women, including Mrs. Proctor, after a couple of false starts, boarded the National City and Otay railcars at 9:00 a.m. They were met at the final station by their guides, with burros for the participants to ride. (The women, of course, rode sidesaddle.) In addition to the local residents and a couple of dignitaries, Mrs. Proctor's brother, John Thompson, had come from Missouri to join her. Four participants turned back before the summit, but for those who made it, Isham had sent his people ahead to set up a flagpole and cannon, two hot air balloons and a picnic table. He had also set up two large tents, one for the men and one for the ladies, for participants to freshen up.

Mrs. Proctor raised the flag, and a minister gave a short speech. Mrs. Proctor demurred as to making a final choice of the location, since she needed to do further study. The planned activities included setting off the Vesuvius-inspired fireworks for the Independence Days festivities, but as anybody who ever lived in San Diego knows, July 4 can be a lovely summer evening or a "you can't see your hand in front of your face" foggy night. Unfortunately, on that night, after a lovely catered dinner, the fog came in and completely obscured not only the surrounding communities' view of the fireworks on the top of San Miguel Mountain but also the campers'

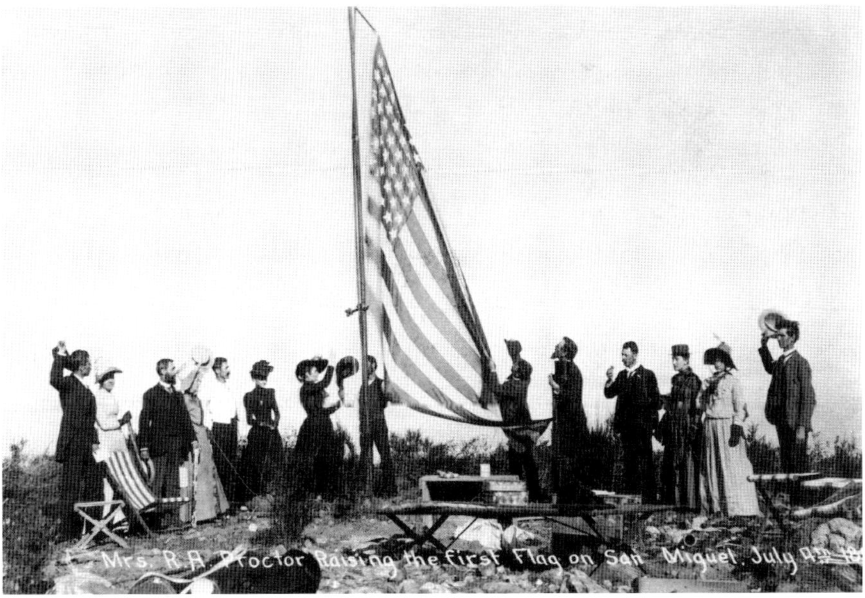

The flag raising on the top of San Miguel Mountain on July 4, 1890. Mrs. Richard Proctor is likely the woman standing to the left of the flagpole. *San Diego History Center.*

ability to even see the stars. After the trip down the next day, Mrs. Proctor vowed to return later in the summer, which she did, spending a week taking sightings from a three-inch telescope. By the end of the week, she tentatively decided to go forward with the observatory on the mountain. She agreed to raise the funds to pay to equip the institution if the city would provide the buildings.

Just six months later, Sallie Proctor wasn't as gung-ho about the project as she had been, which may have something to do with her awareness of Alfred Isham's growing legal issues. Isham had engaged in some unscrupulous business practices, which brought him to court several times for nonpayment of his obligations, which totaled over $15,000 by 1890. In fact, in 1891, Sallie announced a new plan to build an observatory in Mission Heights for which she would give lectures to raise the funds. By 1892, Sallie had married James C. Smythe in Belfast, Ireland. Her ardor for the project did not abate; though she distanced herself from Isham, she continued to work for the idea of a memorial telescope for the next few years.

Isham, who still owned the land on the top of San Miguel, however, continued to push the idea on his own. In 1895, he incorporated the World Proctor Memorial Association, using Proctor's still bankable name, with a project bigger than ever, including two telescopes, one designed by Louis Gathmann, inventor of the sectional lens, to be the largest observatory in the world. In 1896, Isham planned to travel to see Sallie in Belfast and convince her of his sincerity, with a swing through Washington, D.C., on his way, to call on government representatives for their cooperation. Sallie continued to give her lectures until after the turn of the century, but no memorial observatory was built for her husband. In 1941, she died in Ireland. In 1908, a sixty-inch telescope—the largest in the world at the time—opened on Los Angeles's Mount Wilson. Mount Wilson, at over 5,700 feet, is twice as tall as San Miguel.

Isham, who had started marketing his California Waters of Life in 1892, continued to grow that business though he returned to live in New York in 1898. The water, which Isham advertised as a cure for everything from baldness to cancer, was bottled at the base of San Miguel Mountain through a deal he had reached with the owner of the land and was sold across the country. He continued selling water, though he was slowed by an article in *Collier's Magazine* directed at the patent medicine industry that highlighted his false advertising claims. The piece called the water "a fairly good mineral water…and no more useful." In 1910, Isham—heavily in debt—died in New York, and San Miguel remained undeveloped.

In the spring of 1893, a local farmer, Z.M. Potter, planted 160 acres of his land near the base of the mountain with mustard. Zephaniah Murray Potter had come from Nova Scotia to California in 1882. He arrived as a boot maker but was soon occupied as a farmer in San Bernardino. In 1892, he bought 160 acres from the U.S. government near the west side of the base of San Miguel. He was of the opinion that he could take in sixty-five tons of mustard seed from the land, which would have made him a handsome profit at the going rate of eight cents a pound. His belief was that mustard was well suited to the rocky, dry conditions of the area. He acquired enough seed to make some jars of mustard, which he took to the local newspapers as advertising. However, by the fall, it was apparent that his crop had failed and he had "enough mustard seed to make a few plasters for his family, but no more," in the words of a local newspaper. Thus ended the reign of the Mustard King of San Miguel, though the wild mustard continues to bloom every spring on the mountain.

Though Alfred Isham and Sallie Proctor went their separate ways, the idea of building an observatory on San Miguel Mountain continued to reoccur until the 1910s. In addition to the idea of mining the top of the mountain for an observatory, there have been other attempts to mine the mountain. In the summer of 1895, there was the uncovering of an ancient road that the discoverers thought would lead them to a gold mine, though no mine or gold was ever found. In 1900, a corporation was organized to drill for oil at the base of the mountain, but the only thing from out of the ground in or around San Miguel Mountain was the water at Isham's spring. The mountain appears to have a penchant for attracting crackpots.

In 1903, Sam Williams bought a large portion of land at the base of the mountain and started a dairy, the earliest commercial dairy in Bonita. Williams became a respected member of the community, and because of the extensive land he had for grazing, he spent less to buy feed for his dairy cows. On his ranch, he planted a small orchard of citrus, some of which remain on the south side of the Sweetwater Reservoir. Locals continued to hunt on San Miguel, bringing in deer on a regular basis as late as the 1960s, and reports of mountain lions were not uncommon.

Other than the cows of the Williams dairy and regular visits by local children out for a weekend hike, San Miguel Mountain remained a quiet place for over twenty years. Outside of this little quiet quarter of the world time moved on, including the invention and improvement of the airplane. In the mid-1920s, Standard Oil of California constructed a series of five high-intensity aviation beacons to aid pilots in night flying, a boon to the Department of Commerce in setting up air routes. Standard Oil decided to place one of them on top of San Miguel Mountain, though it had also considered Soledad Mountain, Cowles Mountain and Mount Helix. Construction began in the late spring of 1928. At the time, there was no road that led to the base of the mountain, so they had to build one. From the end of the road, the pieces were sledded a mile and a half up the slope using mules, each piece requiring one or two days to complete the journey. Pack animals were also required for provisions for the crew. The installation also necessitated the addition of power to the mountain, so crews from San Diego Consolidated Gas and Electric installed two and a half miles of power poles up the north side of the mountain.

When completed, the ten million–candlepower beacon, built by Sperry Gyroscope Company, topped a twenty-five-foot-high tower, placed on the westernmost of the two summits of the mountain. The rotating light made one complete revolution every ten seconds. On October 14, 1928, the beacon was dedicated, with the neon letters S and M for Standard-Miguel, not San Miguel as is often assumed. (The Portland beacon, SO for Standard-Oregon, and the Seattle beacon, which was SW for Standard-Washington, were also turned on at the same time.) The red neon letters also flashed the Morse code for SM eleven and a half times each minute. All three state governors—C.C. Young of California, I.L. Patterson of Oregon and R.H. Hartely of Washington—touched a telegraph key in their home states to turn on the lights. The ceremony was broadcast live on the NBC radio network.

The light was attended by an operator who lived somewhere near the bottom of the mountain. In addition to fixing malfunctions, the caretaker also was required to repair damage by hooligans who shot out the reflector or stole the lamps. In 1931 and 1932, the lamps were stolen three times, all on foggy nights when the beacons were most important. There was still no road to the top, so the caretaker had to climb the mountain on foot to make repairs. There were multiple reports of boats at sea using the San Miguel beacon for navigation, one of which saw the flashing light from over two hundred miles away, though navigation books warned seamen that they should not mistake the SM beacon for one of the local lighthouses, at their own peril.

In the wake of the attack at Pearl Harbor, the beacon was turned off. There were talks of relighting the beacon after the war, but wartime improvements in aviation made the beacons obsolete. We don't know exactly when the tower was torn down, but a newspaper article from 1959

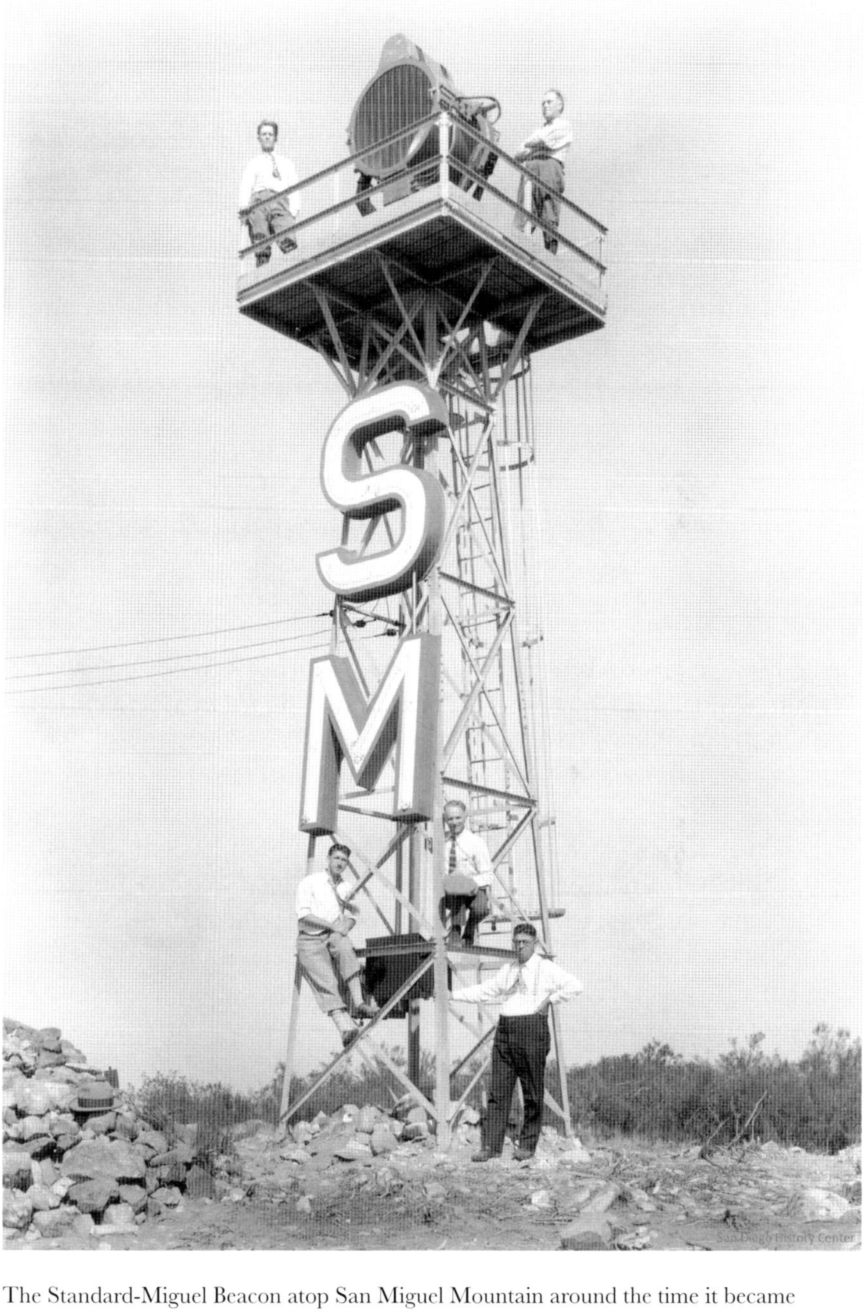

The Standard-Miguel Beacon atop San Miguel Mountain around the time it became operational in 1928. *San Diego History Center.*

indicated the tower was still standing, though the beacon and the power wires had been removed.

It didn't remain quiet on the mountain for long. In 1952, local television station KFMB and radio station KFSD cooperatively purchased the summit of San Miguel Mountain from Standard Oil for use as a transmitter site. KFMB and KFSD intended to move their transmitters from Mount Soledad in La Jolla. It took a while for the first transmitter to be built, but by the early 1960s, several stations were transmitting from San Miguel. In 1969, KCST (now KNSD) even decorated its TV transmission tower with Christmas lights as a gift to San Diego.

Mother Nature has also made appearances on San Miguel Mountain, mostly in the form of brush fires. Most of the early fires were fought by the U.S. Forest Service with hand pumps and bulldozers, hoping to keep fire from burning homes or barns. In 1953, the service fought a two-hundred-acre blaze started by a boy who was separated from his companions and set a fire in hopes of being found. The 1970 Laguna fire burned the eastern and northern side of San Miguel but was stopped before it burned over the top, though that was far from certain in the heat of the fight. The most recent fire on the mountain happened on October 22, 2007, when the Harris fire burned across the top of San Miguel. Spectacular photos of the firestorm on San Miguel show crimson flames atop the mountain, silhouetted against the night sky. The local power lines and poles were burned through around midnight, and KNSD, KPBS, KSWB and KUSI TV stations and KPBS radio lost power. Most of the stations were eventually able to broadcast using backup generators, but the KPBS station didn't have a backup generator. Low-power TV station KSDX had its building completely destroyed, and KPBS radio moved its feed broadcast on another frequency so that it could continue to report on the fire. The blaze burned to the south side of the Sweetwater Reservoir and to vacant graded lots that acted like a firebreak in the Bela Lago neighborhood of Chula Vista before this flank of the fire was stopped. (The eastern portion of Sunnyside was also evacuated during the Harris fire.) Today, in addition to the cellular tower added to the top of the mountain, KPBS, KNSD, KUSI and KSWB still broadcast from San Miguel, as well as several radio stations.

In addition to fire, snow has also blanketed the top of San Miguel. At barely 2,500 feet and just over 10 miles from the ocean, snow has been a rare occurrence, but it happened at least four times in recorded history. The last time snow was recorded there was in 1949.

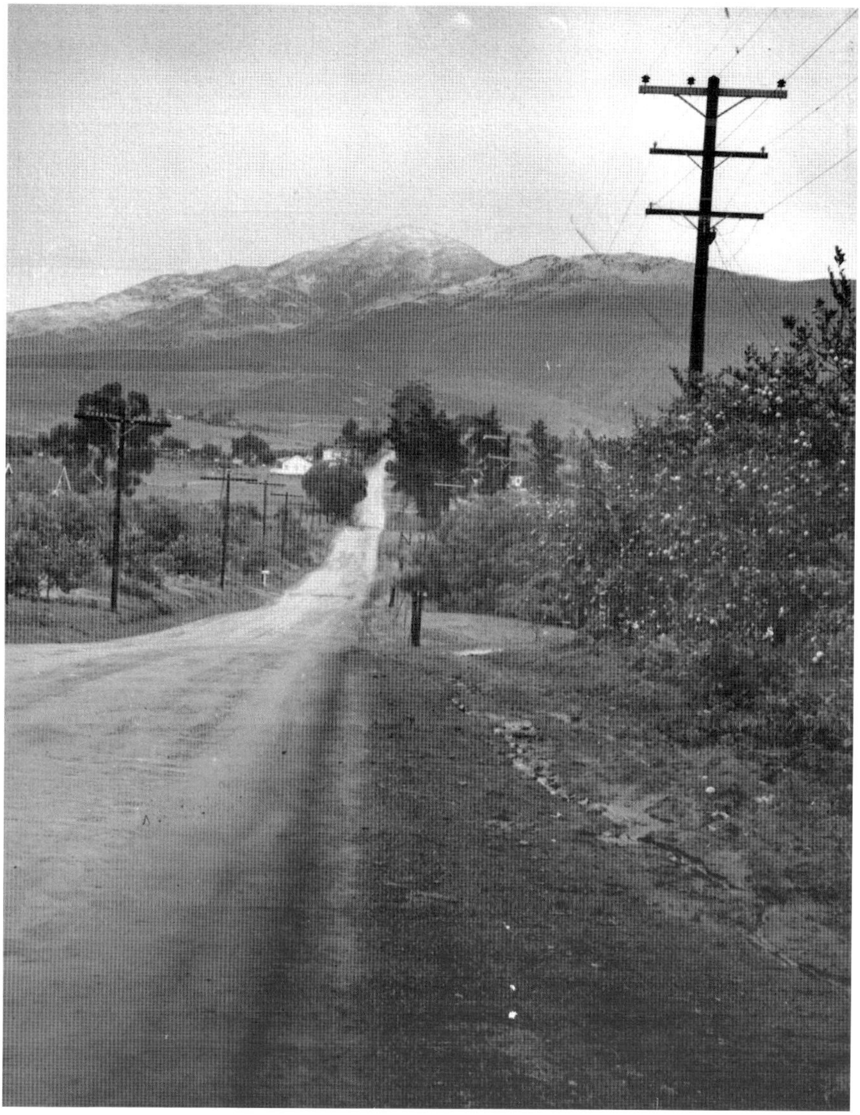

A rare photo of San Miguel Mountain with snow, probably from the 1930s. *Bonita Museum & Cultural Center.*

The intrepid hiker can still climb to the top of San Miguel Mountain, and the reward is a fabulous view of the entire South Bay as well as the northern portion of Mexico. The only permanent fixtures on the mountain are the transmitter towers, though there is now a road to the top. The view from the top of San Miguel Mountain is just about the only thing that still remains the same as 150 years ago when the first Europeans got a chance to reach the summit. If you hike in the late winter or spring, you can look for San Miguel Mountain sage, a native plant that grows only in the South Bay. The light-blue flowers bloom as early as February. The sage plant is still growing on the mountain after so many other attempts to improve the mountain have failed. The schemers and the crackpots have all gone.

3
A HISTORY OF THE BONITA STORE AND ITS PROPRIETORS

When the Sweetwater Fruit Company started operation in Bonita in 1890, the only building standing in the valley that wasn't a dwelling was the schoolhouse. There was no post office, and there was no place to buy or sell goods of any kind. There were people who lived in the valley, and more came to work at the packing house and in the orchards, but they had to make an arduous trip to National City to buy anything or get their mail.

In 1891, a small wooden building was erected right next to the railroad tracks. The earliest photo we know of dates from after the post office was opened in the store in 1898, and the sign displays the name Bonita Store. From the other signs visible in that photo, we know that the store sold groceries, notions, seed, coal and gasoline. It also acted as the Bonita Station for the National City and Otay Railroad. Descriptions from the time mention that the rear portion of the building was a small residence for the proprietor and his or her family.

The property records indicate that the store was built on property owned by the Sweetwater Fruit Company and funded by the various investors involved in the company, at least in part for their own convenience. The company hired the various managers who ran the store and post office.

Now you might ask—why does it matter who ran the store? Were these people important? No and yes. No, most of them didn't ever become famous or even infamous. But they came to Bonita from far and near, and many became treasured members of the community. And as the store was the only business in Bonita until after World War II and all mail had to be picked up at the post office, everyone who lived in the valley interacted with proprietors. It was a one-stop shop because it was the only shop around.

The first proprietor that we know about was Ernest P. Walters with his wife, Ilda. E.P. had worked at an ostrich farm on Coronado in 1892 and later as a store clerk in Escondido. Just prior to taking over the Bonita Store, he was a clerk at Mulvey Bros Grocery in San Diego, located on Market Street in the IOOF building, which still stands. John Mulvey opened his store in the 1880s, but by the 1890s it was being run by his sons, Arthur and Edward, as Mulvey Bros. Mulvey Bros. was a large grocery and mercantile operation, which would have given E.P. sufficient experience to run the small store in Bonita.

Ilda was appointed the first postmaster in 1898. (Though postmistress is often seen, the official title has always been postmaster.) Sunnyside had a post office as early as 1892, but it was two miles up the valley, not convenient to the Allen family and the Sweetwater Fruit Company operation in the era before cars. We know that Ilda had been in San Diego for several years before she married E.P. Compensation for the postmaster was based on commission on postage sales and rentals on the post boxes. This would have been a tidy regular income for anyone willing to oversee the mail. Ilda's compensation was $135 for her year of service in 1898–99. Somewhat abruptly, Ilda resigned her position in May 1899, and Russell C. Allen was appointed the new postmaster, a position he held until 1914. In 1900, Ilda, now relocated to Los Angeles, living with her mother and working as a tailor, was granted a divorce from E.P. on the grounds of desertion. E.P.'s whereabouts are unknown, as he disappeared from the record as well.

Edson O. Parker was a completely different type of man from his predecessor. He was a veteran of the Civil War, founder of a town in South Dakota and survivor of a family tragedy. Edson was born in New York in 1843 and spent three years as a bugler in the Civil War. After the war, from 1867 to 1869, he was postmaster of Jasper, Iowa, where he met and married his wife, Maria. In 1882, he acquired forty acres in the Dakota Territory and set about creating the town of Highmore. He served as postmaster there from 1882 to 1884, in addition to running a loan office and serving several terms as registrar of deeds. He was well known as a dairy man and regularly gave a talk he titled "The Cow Pays the Mortgage," on the effective management of cows and farm debt. Maria contributed to the family income by decorating and selling ladies' hats. Edson opened a grocery in January 1896 and was elected to the South Dakota state legislature that same year, an

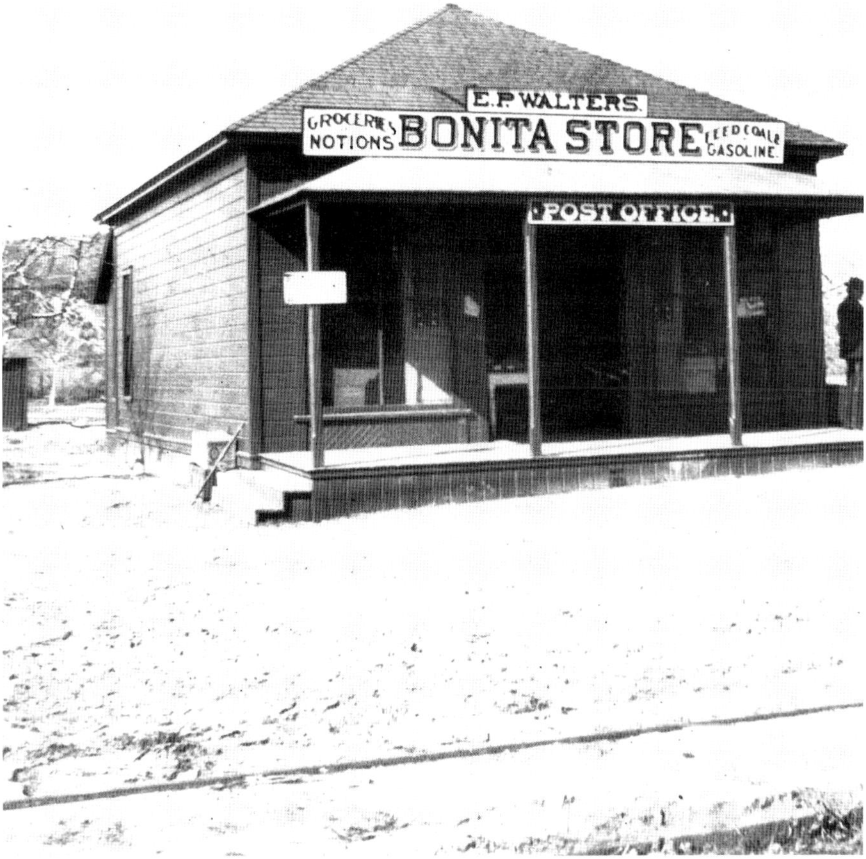

The Bonita Store during E.P. Walters's proprietorship around 1899. The National City & Otay Railroad tracks can be seen near the bottom of the image. *Bonita Museum & Cultural Center.*

honor in any era. However, in December 1896, Maria was washing ribbons in gasoline and water. (Yes, that was the way to wash silk ribbons in the days before dry cleaning.) She had an open gas container next to the wood-burning stove, and the fumes caught fire. She was enveloped in flames before she knew what happened. Grace and Ralph, her children, also were burned, likely trying to save her. She died the next morning after twenty-two hours of "fearful suffering" as the *Sioux Falls Argus-Leader* reported. In the fall of 1897, Edson sold the grocery store, and after completing his service in the legislature, he, Ralph and Grace left for California. It is understandable that the family would want to leave the tragedy behind, though we do not know why they came to California specifically.

Edson, Ralph and Grace took over the Bonita Store in 1899. Edson became postmaster in Bonita in 1901, though, since no official record exists, it may have been just an interim posting or he may have been being paid by Russell Allen to act in his stead. After he left the Bonita Store in 1904, Edson remained in San Diego selling real estate. He died in 1913 and was buried at Mt. Hope Cemetery in the Grand Army of the Republic plot. Grace married William D. Almond, who was living at the boardinghouse on the Sweetwater Fruit Company property adjacent to the store. The Almond family ended up living with Edson for a time around 1910 before moving back to the Sweetwater Valley. Ralph married and moved to Idaho to raise sheep but later returned to San Diego.

From 1903 to 1907, Burton and Effie Forbes ran the Bonita Store. He came from Kansas to San Diego before 1894 and clerked for several grocers in San Diego, including Nason & Company and G.A.L. Urban. He also owned an interest in another grocery in San Diego, which he sold in 1901. After arriving in San Diego, he met and married Effie V. Moore in 1901. Effie had come to California from Texas in 1887 with her parents. She had previously worked as a bookkeeper, a skill that came in handy when operating the Bonita Store. Their daughter, Virginia, was born in 1902, and the Forbeses took over running the store late in 1903, and ran it until 1907, when they moved to National City. In 1907, Effie's sister, Claudia, married George Campbell, who was the foreman at the Sweetwater Fruit Company packing house. Virginia and her parents came back to Bonita often to visit the Campbells, who built a house on the hill above the Bonita Store in 1920. Burton Forbes went into the real estate business, building a small development on National Avenue in 1914. Effie took her bookkeeping experience and started her own business, Mrs. Forbes Pure Horseradish. Though Burton did most of the work, including buying, cleaning, preparing and bottling the horseradish, Effie had the copyright, so to speak, and made the profits. Burton and Effie are interred at Greenwood Memorial Park.

Late in 1907, Samuel Carder Smith took over running the store. Smith was one of four brothers (three born in Indiana and S. Carder, as he was known, in Iowa) who had come to Southern California in the 1880s. Smith operated as a money lender. He was caught up in a forgery case, where he

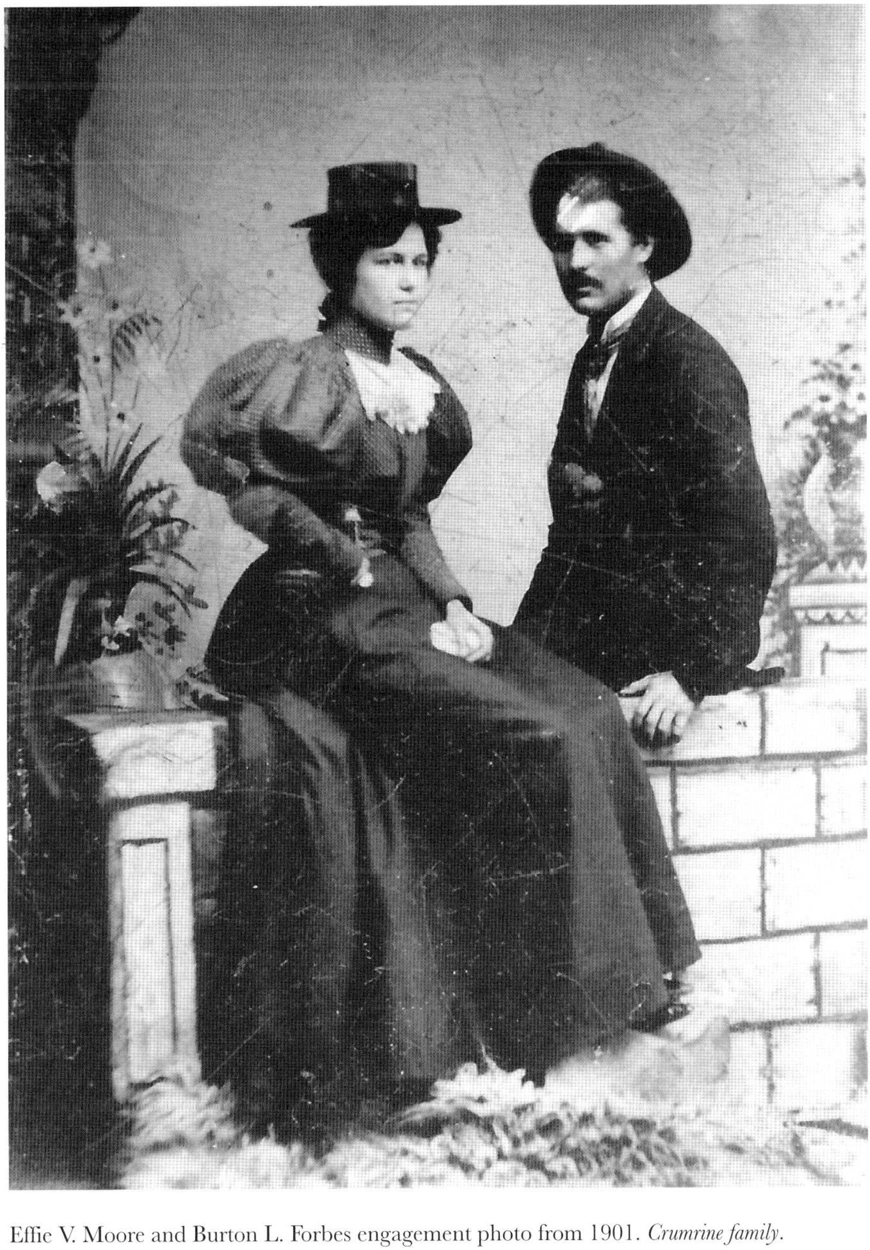

Effie V. Moore and Burton L. Forbes engagement photo from 1901. *Crumrine family.*

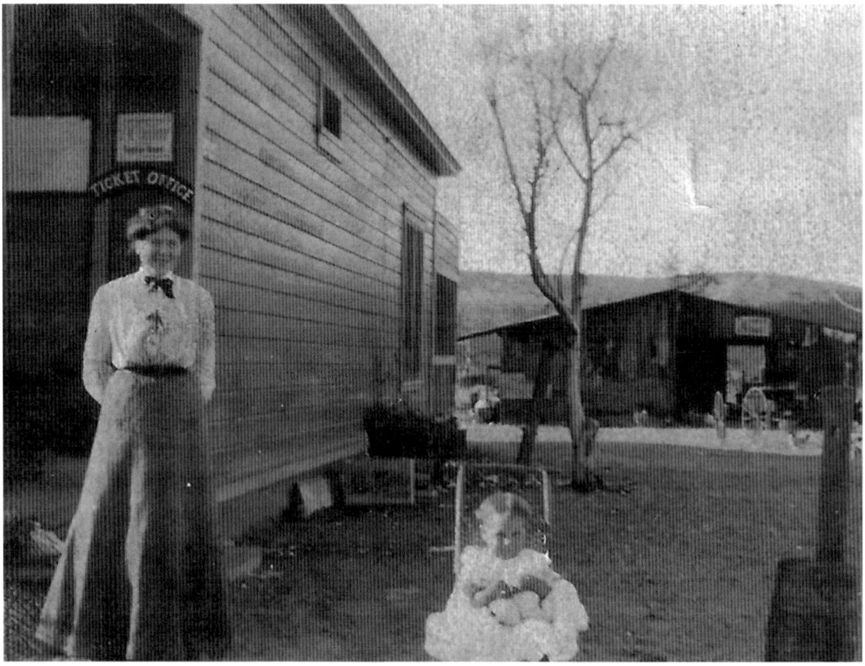

Effie V. Forbes and her daughter Virginia standing on the east side of the Bonita Store around 1903. *Crumrine Family*.

lent money based on completed timecards that turned out to be forgeries. The case was eventually dismissed (largely because the mastermind died), and Smith went on to sell questionable products like Potter's Perfect Purifier (a coal-tar disinfectant) and cures for stomach ailments and catarrh from Copa de Oro, as well as acting as a property broker. He left the Bonita Store after less than a year and moved on to running the store and being postmaster in Bernardo. He later ran afoul of the law there when he tried to open an establishment selling liquor, for which he was fined $300. He was known for frequently writing letters to the paper about local issues.

The replacement for S. Carder Smith was the Bushnell family—mother Jessie, son Ralph and daughter Mabel. The family (including another daughter, Ethel) came from South Dakota, where Jessie had been married to Edward Bushnell. Edward left for the gold strike in the Yukon and never returned, leaving Jessie in quite a quandary, so she loaded the kids up in a wagon and headed for California. They arrived in San Diego before 1900, where Mabel worked at Marston's Department Store, and Ralph worked in a dry goods store in downtown San Diego.

In August 1905, daughter Ethel, who had trained to be a nurse, married Dr. George Barrow Worthington. She met the doctor during her training at St. Luke's Hospital. Dr. Worthington became the resident doctor in Chula Vista, though his main office was in downtown San Diego. In 1912, the Worthingtons built El Nido, one of the historic homes in Chula Vista.

During the Bushnells' time running the store, Ralph operated a Wells Fargo office. From 1852 to 1918, Wells Fargo operated an express service for rapid delivery of gold, mail and valuables. By 1918, Wells Fargo had become part of ten thousand communities across the country. The Wells Fargo express service officially ended in 1918, when at the behest of the secretary of the treasury, the three big express companies in the country were merged into the American Railway Express "in the interests of winning" World War I. Ralph ended his relationship with Wells Fargo in 1912 when the Bushnells left the store.

Mabel moved back and forth between her mother and married sister's home. George and Ethel lived in Chula Vista until 1940. In 1914–15, Ralph moved to Mesa Grande, California, with his mother and Mabel, where he raised cattle and may have been involved with a tourmaline mine. Jessie died in San Diego in June 1934.

In 1912, Wood G. Berkey took over the Bonita store with his partner Richard L. Newcomb. Wood and his wife, Mary, had been living in San Diego since at least 1905, where he had been a clerk at a furniture store. Newcomb was a clerk at the Hotel del Coronado and then at San Diego Post Office prior to their partnership. In 1913, Newcomb became the postmaster in Sunnyside, as the men split the duties of running both stores. In 1914, Newcomb left the partnership to work at the post office in El Paso, Texas. To fill the void, Wood's brother Howard H. and his wife, Agnes, arrived in town from Indiana, where they had been living with Wood and Howard's parents. Howard and Agnes took over running the Sunnyside store, where Howard was soon named postmaster.

In January 1916, the floods that devastated the valley also affected the Bonita Store. The building sustained some damage to its foundations, but it was not completely washed away. With train service removed from the valley, proximity to the tracks was less of a priority, and the wooden building was moved to the east, to a spot near the Bonita Schoolhouse, and reoriented to face north. Howard and Agnes left in 1919 and moved to Elsinore but returned to the valley in 1933. In 1937, they built a new home in Edward Anderson and Algot Swanson's Sunny Vista development near Chula Vista. In 1922, Wood and Mary left Bonita for Fresno, where they ran a general merchandise store.

The Haffly family arrived in Bonita in 1920 with their son, Allen. The family came from Pennsylvania, where Charles was postmaster of Kilmer in May 1900. In 1904, the family moved to Flagstaff, Arizona, where Charles began a series of jobs, starting with the forest service, with which he was stationed at Rogers Lake. In 1907, Charles moved to the Hercules Mercantile in Kelvin and later to Tempe Hardware, then to the reclamation service at Granite Reef Dam, where he was camp steward. In 1910, the family was living in Gila, Arizona, where Charles was a clerk in a commissary near where the U.S. government was building Roosevelt Dam. By 1911, the family had moved to Coronado where Charles was first a clerk at the Coronado Lumber Company in 1912 and then bookkeeper there in 1914–16. The family arrived in Bonita in 1920, and Charles was appointed postmaster in 1921. After so many moves, the Hafflys remained at the store for a decade and stayed in the valley after leaving the store. Emma was widely known as a music teacher and played the piano for many weddings and other occasions in the valley as well as at the Friends Church.

Sometime in the late 1920s, the Sweetwater Fruit Company decided to upgrade the store building. The wooden structure was over thirty years old and lacked the space for modern refrigeration and other amenities. The company took advantage of the property it owned along Bonita Road and built the new store farther west, where the Willow Street Bridge intersects Bonita Road. The new stucco building with a tile roof was larger and had modern gas pumps alongside. It also contained a small residence at the back for the manager.

The next proprietors of the Bonita Store were Frank and Lona Vaughan, who took over the store in 1930, when Frank also became postmaster. (As a younger man, he had been a mail carrier.) The Vaughans came to San Diego from Illinois in 1927, after their children were grown. The local community didn't get to know the couple well, because their time in Bonita was cut short when Lona died on Christmas Eve 1932. Frank resigned his position by May 1933 and moved in with his son and family in San Diego.

Benjamin and Laura White took over the store in the wake of Frank Vaughn's departure, and Benjamin was appointed postmaster in September 1933. Frank and Laura had farmed in Nebraska and Idaho before arriving in El Cajon in the mid-1920s, where they farmed on the Ivanhoe Ranch. Laura had been a teacher in Kansas before they were married, a job she loved but had to leave after contracting typhoid fever in 1909. The Whites lived in a home in Lincoln Acres while running the store, which they did until the spring of 1941, just before the start of World War II.

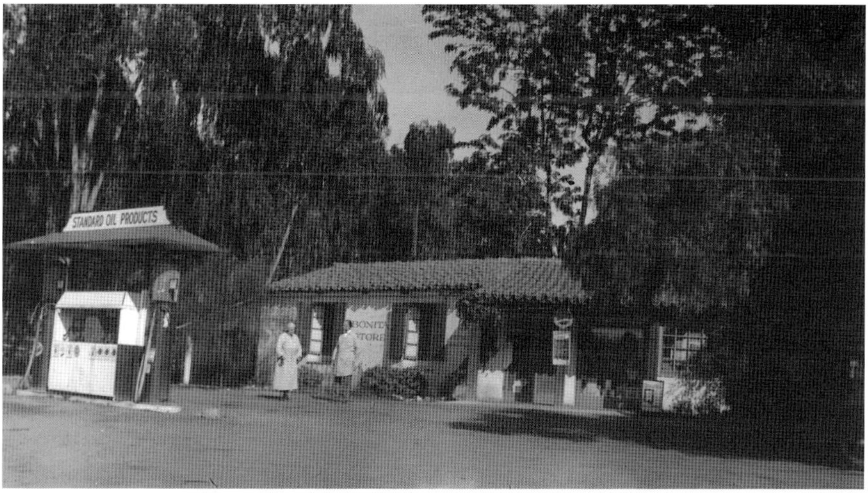

Laura and Benjamin White standing in front of the Bonita Store in the 1930s, this being the new building built in the late 1920s. *Bonita Museum & Cultural Center.*

In July 1941, Michael J. "Mickey" and Thelma F. O'Brien moved to Bonita with their children Patricia and James, and Thelma was appointed postmaster. She had previously assisted at the post office in Palm City and National City, and Mickey had been an employee at Glen Abbey, a job he left to take over managing the store. At the age of sixteen, Mickey came to the United States from Ireland to live with his sister and arrived in San Diego in the early 1930s.

During World War II, things were quiet in the valley, though the Bonita Post Office was reclassified as a third-class office in 1945 based on increased local sales. The influx of people prompted the owners of the Sweetwater Fruit Company to wonder if they needed to increase services. And the year after the war ended, they did just that. In November 1946, La Tienda opened, just to the east of the Bonita Store. Billed as "Bonita's Most Modern Building," La Tienda offered a soda fountain, sundries, hardware, paint and sporting goods. Mickey O'Brien took over managing La Tienda as well as the Bonita Store. In 1947, he left the stores and went to work managing National Motor Sales in National City, which later became McCune Motors. Wes Hebdon took over managing the store, and Lorene Pickering took over as acting postmaster, ending the trend of store managers also overseeing the post office. (Lorene continued to work at the post office as a clerk after the next postmaster was appointed, winning a superior service award from the U.S. Post Office Department in 1967.)

In the spring of 1950, the Bonita Store, which had been in operation since the late 1920s, underwent a major renovation. The portion of the building that faced Bonita Road originally featured a covered walkway. During the renovation, that walkway was enclosed and fronted with redwood and large glass windows, bringing daylight into what had been a somewhat dark space. The store also got new vegetable counters, and a new freezer and food dispensers, making the store as up-to-date as its neighbor, La Tienda. The manager, Wes Hebdon, called it a "complete, moderate-price grocery." The Bonita Post Office remained in the store, receiving a minor update, with Josephine Loomis taking over as postmaster, a job that she would keep for fifteen years.

In 1950, the remaining members of the family company—Richard M. Allen, Mary A. Ward, Meredith L. Campbell and Edgar D. Boal—decided to sell the Bonita Store, which they had owned since 1892. Wes Hebdon had hoped for a deal to buy the market, but in August, Donald and Rita Stadille bought the Bonita Store. Donald had been managing La Tienda since Mickey O'Brien left and was one of the original volunteers with the Bonita Fire Department in 1950.

By January 1956, the post office had outgrown its space in the store and needed to find a new home. It moved two doors east to the former Sweetwater Fruit Company offices, though it remained a third-class office by sales. This move did, however, open up some much-needed space in the Bonita Store. The Stadilles decide to retire to Northern California, and their going-away party at the Sunnyside Steak Ranch was "standing room only" in May 1957.

In April 1957, George and Helen Dull bought the store with George's brother Glen. George and Glen had run meat departments and markets in Texas before coming to California, and they were soon well known by valley residents for their time behind the butcher counter at the store. In 1959, Glen had major heart surgery, though he did return to work within a couple of months. The Bonita Post Office quickly outgrew its new space and, in 1963, moved into the newly renovated La Tienda building. Sales had raised the facility to a second-class position in 1961 (over $10,000 in receipts), which allowed for home delivery to local residents beginning in 1962. Sadly, Glen Dull died in 1966 at age forty-seven, and the next year, George decided to sell the store for the cost of the fixtures and retire.

Joe DiRienzo had been waiting for the Bonita Store to come up for sale. When he saw the small announcement in the classified section of the paper, he drove directly to the store and banged on the door, but no one was there.

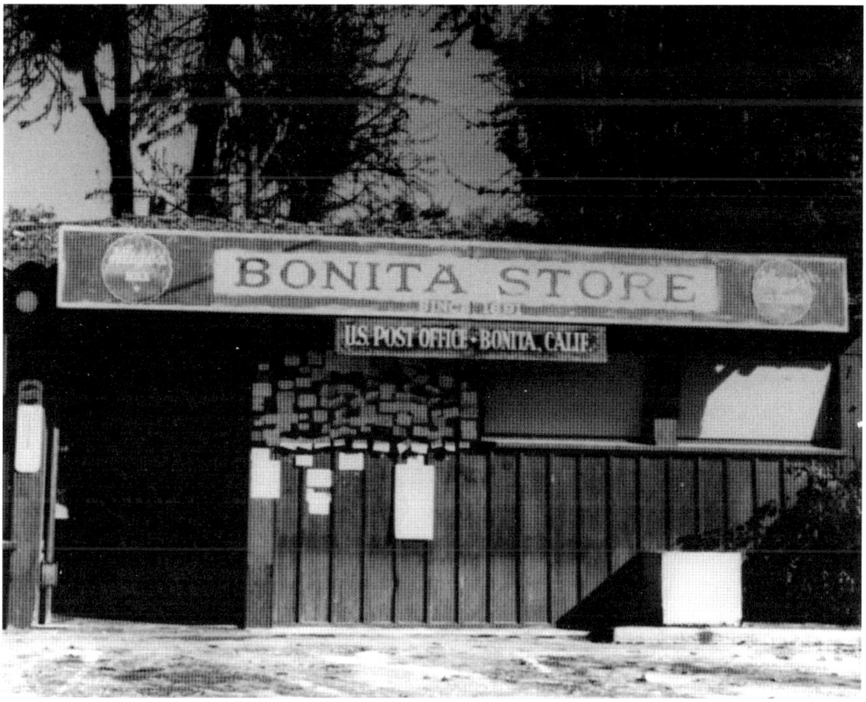

The front door of the Bonita Store after the remodeling in the 1950s but before the Bonita Post Office left in 1956. *Bonita Museum & Cultural Center.*

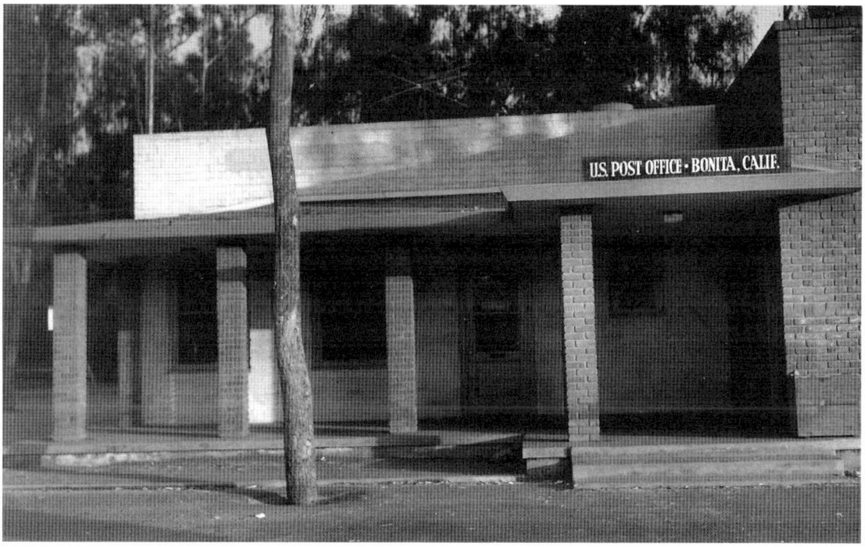

The Bonita Post Office after its move to the former Sweetwater Fruit Company offices in 1956. *Bonita Museum & Cultural Center.*

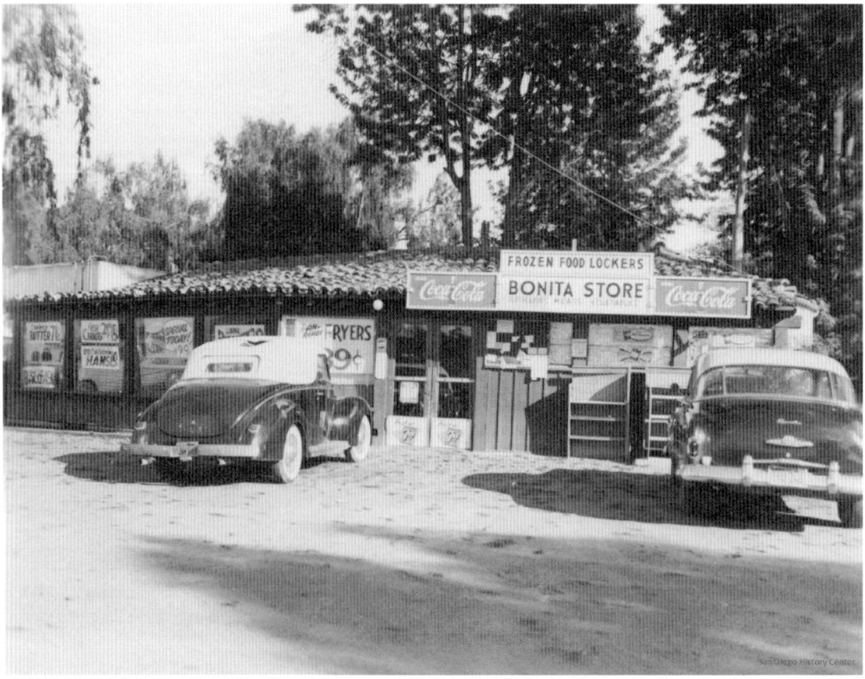

The Bonita Store in January 1957, when the Sweetwater Fruit Company did an appraisal of assets prior to the dissolution of the company. *San Diego History Center.*

He considered waiting through the night, but instead, Joe returned the next day at 7:00 a.m. to get in touch with George Dull. Within minutes, a deal was set, and in February 1967, Joe and his wife, Mary, and their neighbors the Hendersons became the owners of the Bonita Store.

Joe DiRienzo was born in New Jersey, one of eight children born to first-generation Italian American parents. He served in the army in World War II, ending his service in Honolulu, Hawaii. After the war, he and his wife, Mary, moved to Indianapolis, where he had become an executive with General Motors, but Joe really wanted to have a family business just like his parents had, and that brought him to California. Joe and Mary arrived in 1961 and settled in Chula Vista. Prior to buying the Bonita Store, Joe and Mary owned a Speedee Mart store in Chula Vista (this 127-store chain founded by Henry Boney was bought by 7-11 in 1964) as well as a Taco Bell in Imperial Beach.

Joe had a real vision for remaking the establishment into a traditional country store complete with a pot-bellied stove, a pickle barrel and a deli, all things he remembered from his childhood. His father ran the family deli in New Jersey, where he made his own sausage. The DiRienzos engaged local architect Victor Wulff to help them redesign the front of the store and began plans to install a deli featuring homemade and kosher specialties. Joe had also hoped to create a patio space, but that dream would have to wait.

Under Joe and Mary's management, the Bonita Store did well, and in 1970, the DiRienzos built a house on Overlook Court in Sunnyside so they could be closer to their business. Joe introduced hero sandwiches featuring the meats from his deli, many of which were made from his family recipes. Over the years, Joe must've sold thousands of the sandwiches to people in the Sweetwater Valley for birthday parties, pool parties, employee lunches and more. In fact, the sandwiches sold so well that in 1972, Joe opened a sandwich shop on Third Avenue in Chula Vista. That same year, Joe leased a small portion of the Bonita Store to Leanne Kozak to become the Bonita Health Emporium, stocking local honey and grains and natural vitamins to take advantage of the health food craze. As the craze dwindled in the mid-1970s, Kozak left to work in TV news, and the Health Emporium was no more.

Running a country store is not an easy thing, and something happened the year Joe bought the Bonita Store that made it even harder. In December

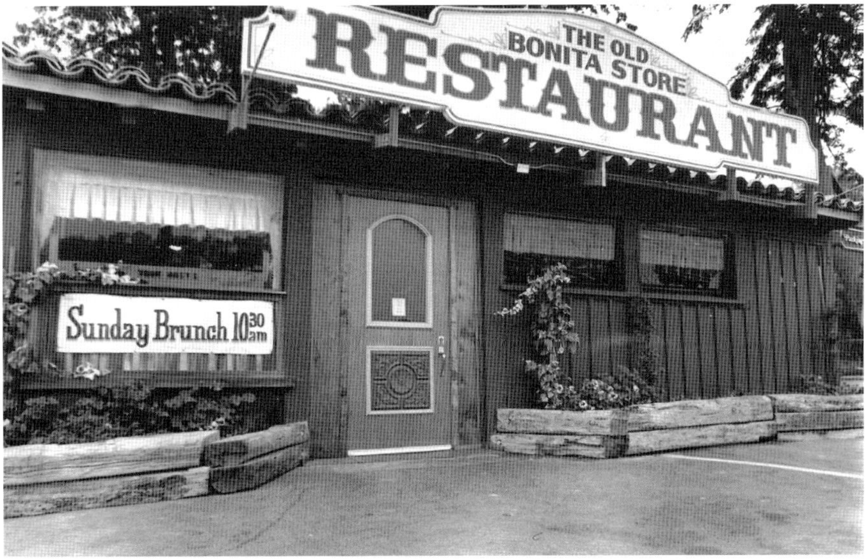

The front door of the Old Bonita Store Restaurant after the remodeling. *Bonita Museum & Cultural Center.*

1967, Big Bear Markets announced that it would bring its eighteenth store in the San Diego region to Bonita. The new store was located at Bonita and Allen School Roads, just a quarter of a mile down the road from the Bonita Store. Though small by today's standards, Big Bear was a full supermarket—it even gave out Green Stamps.

All the love in the world could not keep this small country store operating, and in 1978, Joe announced that the store was going to become the Old Bonita Store Restaurant. Joe and Mary had been doing a lot of catering in the last five years, and with the demise of the Sunnyside Steak Ranch in 1973, Bonita didn't really have a signature place for friends to gather to celebrate. And that was exactly what the DiRienzos wanted to create, especially with their son Rick as manager. Joe threw himself into the renovations just as he had when he originally acquired the store. He wanted the restaurant to have a homey, country vibe. The renovations included installing a kitchen and opening the space that had previously been the attached residence.

In the years of living in Chula Vista, Joe's family had come to enjoy taking trips to Baja, especially stopping for lobster in Puerto Nuevo. Puerto Nuevo–style lobster is pan-fried and served with rice, beans, tortillas and

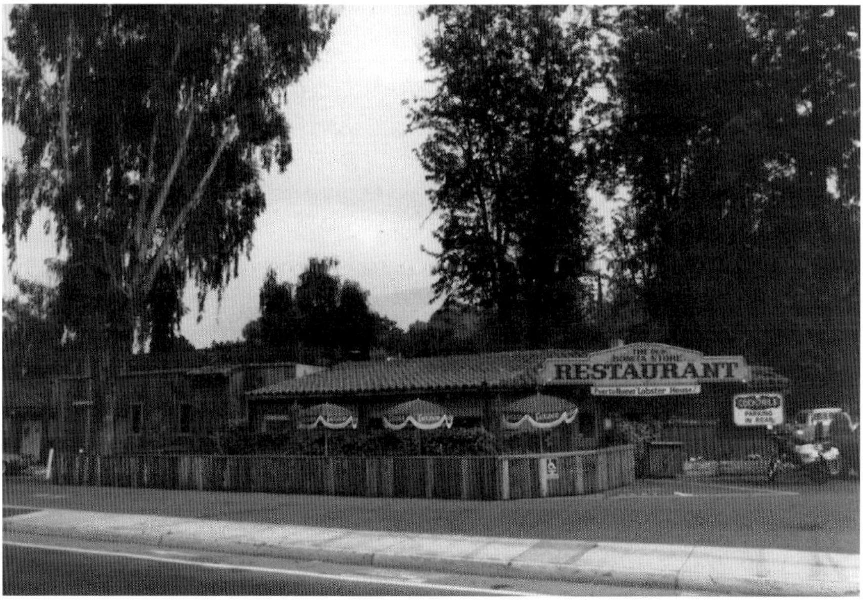

The Old Bonita Store Restaurant after the patio was added. *Bonita Museum & Cultural Center.*

drawn butter. It's a simple preparation, but getting fresh Pacific lobster is the key to being successful. Joe had the contacts to do that, and in 1983, Joe and Rick introduced Puerto Nuevo–style lobster to the Old Bonita Store Restaurant several nights a week. Saturday, Sunday, Monday and Tuesday nights for $9.95, patrons could get lobster and all the fixins' without the drive to Mexico. Within just a month, the lobster was available seven nights a week. Over the years, the restaurant décor transformed to a Mexican cantina look, but the locals still called it the Bonita Store. In 1992, the family opened a Rockin' Baja Lobster restaurant in Oceanside, one of six locations in San Diego and Orange County.

There were ups and downs, but the DiRienzo clan kept things going in Bonita for a long time. Sadly, Joe died in December 2003, and in late 2004, the family decided to sell the Bonita Store location. A new owner took over the space but was not successful, and the building stood empty for many months.

Though the Bonita Store is gone, the building that housed it since the late 1920s is still standing. It's an old building, and it has cost a fair amount to keep it up to the new codes. There have been rumors over the years that the owners would tear it down in favor of a fancy new office building, but that has so far not come to pass. As the oldest commercial building in Bonita, it would be a shame if it was lost for good.

4
THOSE CRAZY MEN AND THEIR FLYING MACHINES

LIGHTER-THAN-AIR CRAFT

Today we take flying for granted, but that wasn't always the case. Though you don't look around Bonita and see evidence of aviation, that doesn't mean there wasn't any. Before airplanes, there were airships. The desire to fly higher or farther took many by storm, and in 1892, it took Robert J. Woodward. His dream was to fly a balloon across the country. Professor Woodward, as he called himself, was a fruit farmer from Ventura who became an aeronaut late in life. He was fifty-five when he relocated to San Diego, and he believed the prevailing winds would take him eastward and that the shorter mountains would be easier to fly over. His intended destination was the East Coast of the United States, which he thought would take three or four days to reach.

Woodward had been fascinated by lighter-than-air-flight for years, but he was introduced to ballooning in 1891 in Midland, Texas. The U.S. Department of Agriculture funded experiments looking into the idea that explosions might cause rain. This theory had grown out of anecdotal information that rain showers often followed large military battles. (No, I'm not kidding.) The U.S. government's representative contracted with Carl Myers of upstate New York to produce exploding balloons for use in testing this theory. Myers had been building balloons since 1878, a craft he got into through his lifelong interest in meteorology. He called his home and factory the Balloon Farm. Through experimentation, Myers had devised a varnish that restricted the loss of hydrogen through the balloon silk, but the chemicals were dangerous enough that the work had to be completed outdoors. Myers said that similar conditions were necessary for balloon making as they were for farming, hence he referred to his setup as a farm. Myers's most well-known contraption was a sky cycle—a sausage-shaped balloon with a basket below—in which he rode over the countryside. We have no idea why Woodward was in Texas, but we do know that is how he came in contact with Carl Myers. (The experiments in causing rain through explosions were less than conclusive.)

Woodward arrived in San Diego in late May 1892 and began making preparations for his trip across the continent. He built scaffolding around an excavation at Eighth and H Streets in San Diego (present-day Eighth and Broadway) and surrounded the scaffolding with canvas to protect the balloon from wind during inflation. The newly purchased balloon (it cost $600) arrived from Myers's Balloon Farm in early June. When filled with twelve thousand cubic feet of gas, it was thirty-six feet high and twenty-six feet wide. From the yellow fabric balloon, covered in a white mesh, dangled a three- by three-foot basket in which Professor Woodward would stand. The basket also included two oars, designed by Woodward, made of bamboo and canvas, roughly two and a half by six feet in length. Woodward believed he could use the oars to both rise and lower the balloon, and they would act as rudders to direct its flight. It was the incorporation of the oars that would require several test flights before Woodward left on his long journey. Woodward believed his extensive skill with oars in the water would translate to his balloon.

In June 1892, Woodward announced his plans to inflate the balloon in downtown San Diego and perform a couple of test flights before heading off on his grand journey. His first attempt did not go well. When he tapped the local hydrogen gas main, he discovered that the gas was entirely too heavy and found that four thousand cubic feet would scarcely lift the balloon from the ground. He initially thought to move the balloon to the gas works but instead went to weigh the gas at the works, finding it wholly unsuitable for lighter-than-air flight. He sent a telegram east to Carl Myers requesting a gas generator, which would delay his trip for a week at least. In addition to Myers's expertise in building his balloon, Woodward also leaned on the local weather officer, Martin L. Hearne, for regular updates on the winds. But since Hearne primarily was a recorder of weather rather than a forecaster, there was only so much help he could give. Woodward planned to telegraph

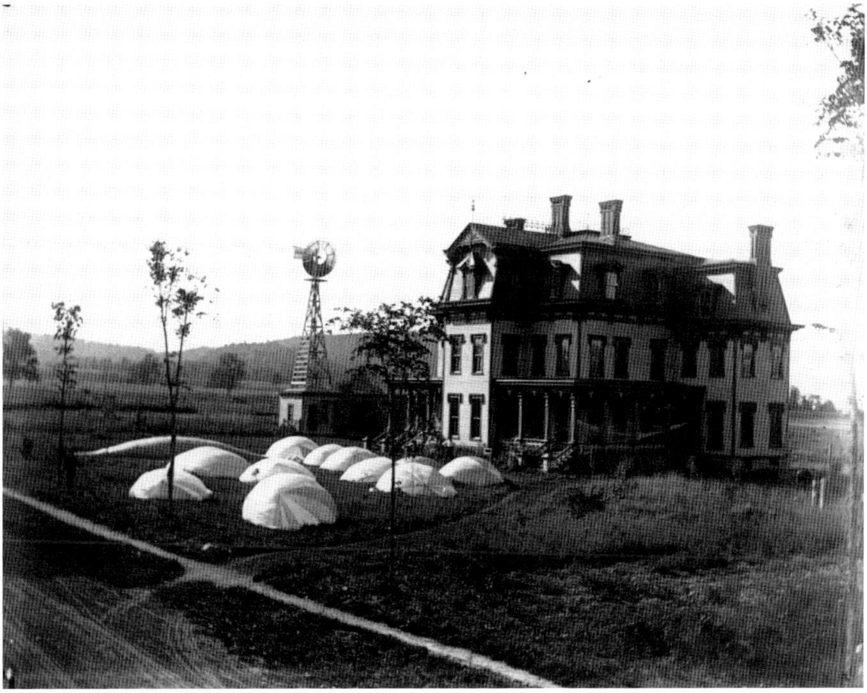

Carl Myers's Balloon Farm in Frankfort, New York, 1892. *Smithsonian National Air and Space Museum (NASM 95-17).*

other weather offices across the country for wind reports before he left. (I have no idea how he planned to update his weather forecasts during his trip.)

On July 13, Woodward was ready to try again after finally receiving his generator and inflating his balloon. Once free of its tethers, the balloon shot up and found a current that headed it toward the ocean. Woodward furiously threw off ballast and rose higher, finding a westerly current. An hour after the ride commenced, Woodward and his balloon disappeared from the view of the assembled crowd in downtown San Diego. He continued easterly for quite a few miles and came to rest in El Cajon. It took him several days to retrieve his balloon and return it to San Diego.

Discouraged after his attempts in San Diego were unsuccessful, Woodward decided to move to Los Angeles to try his luck, hoping to find hydrogen gas with greater lifting capacity. On July 25, when Woodward wanted to complete any early trial of his rig, high winds forced him to abort his flights. On August 6, Woodward attempted to inflate his balloon as part of an experiment in remaining aloft overnight, but the Los Angeles winds were again a problem. Woodward decided to call off the experiment, and while the balloon was being deflated, the silk fabric slipped out of the netting and drifted away. Woodward and his crew had to secure a horse and buggy and follow the balloon across the countryside. It was finally recovered three miles away.

After his initial flights, Woodward realized he would need a larger balloon to complete his trip. This larger balloon, with a capacity of nineteen thousand cubic feet of gas, arrived in San Diego, and Woodward returned to try again. This is where Bonita comes into the story. On August 17, 1892, Woodward, using his larger balloon, set off again to test the lifting power of the gas and whether his "wings" would allow him to control the balloon. He partially filled the balloon to sixteen thousand cubic feet. He took three days of provisions on board—in case of a landing far from civilization—as well as fifteen sacks of ballast. He also took a barometer and thermometer—both had been tested by Martin Hearne. When the tethers were released at 8:30 a.m., the extra ballast meant that he rose slowly and in a much more controlled fashion than his previous flights. He used the wings to minor success, raising and lowering the balloon and directing it in a southwesterly direction for the spectators to see. The balloon continued southerly, nearly reaching the Mexican border before Woodward lowered the trajectory to find a northerly breeze.

He came down by midday near the Bonita Schoolhouse, eventually settling on Edward Wells's land. Woodward threw out the anchor, expecting it to dig in and stop him, but instead, the balloon was dragged nearly three-quarters of a mile. In the process, he crossed a barbed-wire fence and scratched himself, straightened out his anchor, broke up the basket and tore a hole in the balloon. Local ranchers came to his rescue and helped capture the balloon. He was able to catch a National City and Otay train out of the valley and to arrive in San Diego by 5:00 p.m., but after further inspection, the balloon had a severe tear. He planned to take the balloon to Los Angeles for repairs, but we aren't quite sure where the balloon ended up. (It may also have gone to Texas.) Woodward returned to his farm and wife, Amanda, in Ojai. Amanda, who had remained at home, was happy to have Robert indulge his passion, but she wanted no part of witnessing it. Robert found the "air currents on the coast…so baffling as to make his trial uncertain." He died in Los Angeles in 1906 without ever achieving his goal, but for a few weeks in the summer of 1892, it must've been quite exciting to watch the skies over San Diego and Bonita.

Though the Wright brothers did achieve powered flight in 1903, the skies over Bonita remained quiet until the late 1920s. At that time, the sport of gliding became popular in United States. Gliding had become popular in Germany in the years after World War I, when German companies were not allowed to construct high-powered airplanes. By the 1920s, glider enthusiasts were popping up across the United States, primarily building and flying craft of their own designs. In October 1928, Elmore Shoudy, a mechanic, and his partner Russell Winterrowd, a bicycle store owner, flew a small glider they designed in the vicinity of Market Street, not far from Winterrowd's shop on Imperial Avenue. The craft soared about four hundred feet in the air and stayed aloft about five minutes. Shoudy had come to San Diego from Wisconsin, and he had a wife and three children and was employed as a mechanic. An article in the newspaper stated that the two had been working on the glider for almost two years, and Shoudy believed that in the right wind he could stay aloft indefinitely. Shoudy stated for the newspaper that his was going to be the first demonstration of this kind in local aviation history. Local Bonita resident Richard Allen and his friend H. Grafton Chapman helped Shoudy pay for the construction of the glider. Chapman served with the Canadian, British and American forces during World War I as a field lieutenant but had become a civilian pilot after he returned home. He was very interested in gliding.

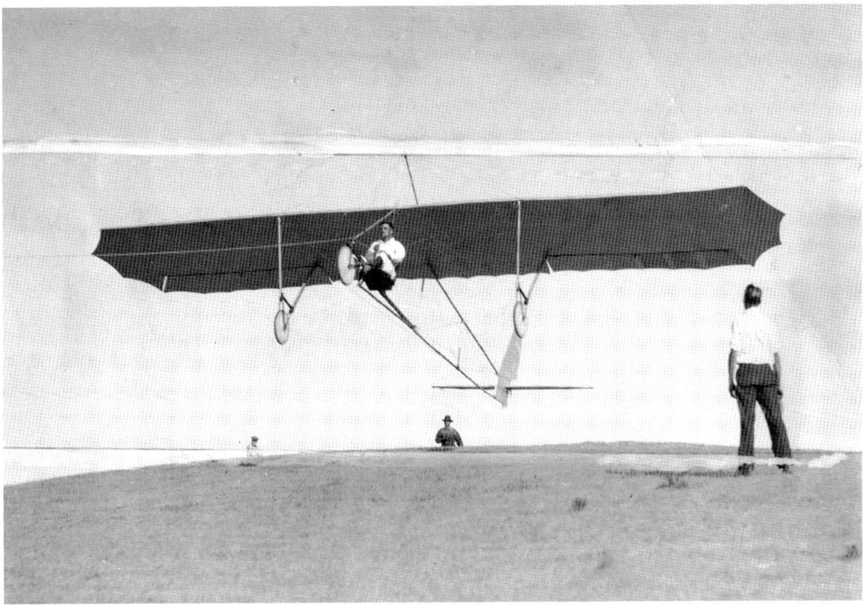

Elmore Shoudy tests his glider in November 1928, a week before his flights in Bonita. *Author's collection.*

Shoudy and his partner had planned this exhibition of gliding to prepare an upcoming local glider meet, the first such meet held in San Diego. It was being sponsored by the Pacific Beach Men's Association and the San Diego Chamber of Commerce in July, and the local glider community was gearing up to participate. (Control of aviation had been placed under the U.S. Department of Commerce because of the Air Commerce Act of 1926.) Shoudy's glider weighed 140 pounds and had a thirty-six-foot wingspan. The entire craft consisted of a large wing, a rudder, three wheels and a small seat for the driver. Shoudy chose a four-hundred-foot hill just behind the Sweetwater Fruit Company orchards (owned by Allen's family) as his launch spot for the demonstration. The hill had a gently sloping top and a dirt access road. Using a car with a tow rope to launch the glider, Shoudy expected to be able to stay aloft for several minutes.

Shoudy and his team arrived early on the morning of December 3 and were able to do several test flights. During those flights, Shoudy decided that the rudder was too small for the control he needed, and he swapped it out for a larger rudder from his shop. A crowd assembled along the top of the hill, and just after 3:00 p.m. Shoudy announced to the crowd, which included his wife and children, that he was ready for his flight. A two-hundred-foot tow rope was attached to the car, which was driven by Chapman. Chapman

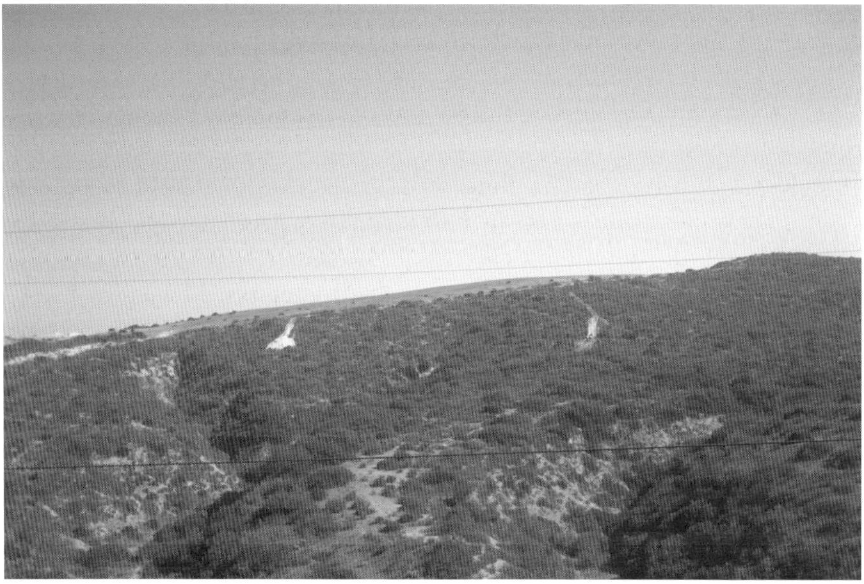

The gently sloping crest of Dead Man's Hill made it an ideal spot for launching Elmore Shoudy's craft. This photo dates to the 1970s. *George E. Oswell.*

drove forward and pulled pilot and glider into the air. Shoudy steered the craft into a northwest wind, but suddenly, the glider lurched. The connector on the tail broke off, and the craft plunged to the earth from seventy-five feet. Shoudy, who was bleeding badly and had broken both his legs, was extricated and died en route to the Paradise Valley sanitarium. The crowd, which included many local Bonita residents, quietly walked down the hill. The local newspaper mistakenly believed that Shoudy's was the first glider fatality in California, but it was not, though it was likely the first glider fatality in San Diego County. Shoudy's unsuccessful flight left its mark on Bonita, however, as from that point forward, the locals referred to the knoll as Dead Man's Hill or Dead Man Mountain.

You might have thought that such an incident would have kept flyers away from Bonita, but that was not the case. Just four months later, William Hawley Bowlus brought his glider, SP-1, to Bonita and made several test flights. Bowlus had made fifteen sailplanes before SP-1, but he had more success with his newest craft. Called Paperwing because the wing ribs were made from craft paper, the plane's body was wood, keeping the weight at 160 pounds. It differed from Shoudy's glider in that its body was enclosed, and Bowlus took the plane to Bonita on several occasions for practice. On April 8, he completed four flights, the longest being a minute and a half. On at least one attempt, he launched his glider from Dead Man's Hill, but his day ended when the wingtips suffered minor damage. On June 29, he even made an attempt to break the existing record of nine minutes and forty-five seconds in an American-designed and built plane (held by the Wright brothers) but failed.

On July 5, Bowlus came in third in a local glider meet held in Pacific Beach, the event in which Shoudy had planned on participating. Bowlus's experience with the upward air currents at the ocean made him change his mind about the location for making his record attempts. Moving to Point Loma in October 1929, he set a new U.S. soaring record of fourteen minutes, ten seconds, launching from a narrow dirt roadway just to the north of the Old Point Loma Lighthouse via a shock cord. Two weeks later, he broke his record by staying aloft one hour and twenty-one minutes.

In the wake of Bowlus's record-breaking success, and with his participation, there was local interest in starting a glider club in Chula Vista. The Chula Vista Glider Club was organized in March 1930, with an advisory committee that included Bowlus and Roland Tyce, owner of the Chula Vista Airport. Bowlus and three other local glider pilots made demonstration flights near Otay as part of the push for the creation of the organization. Even Chula

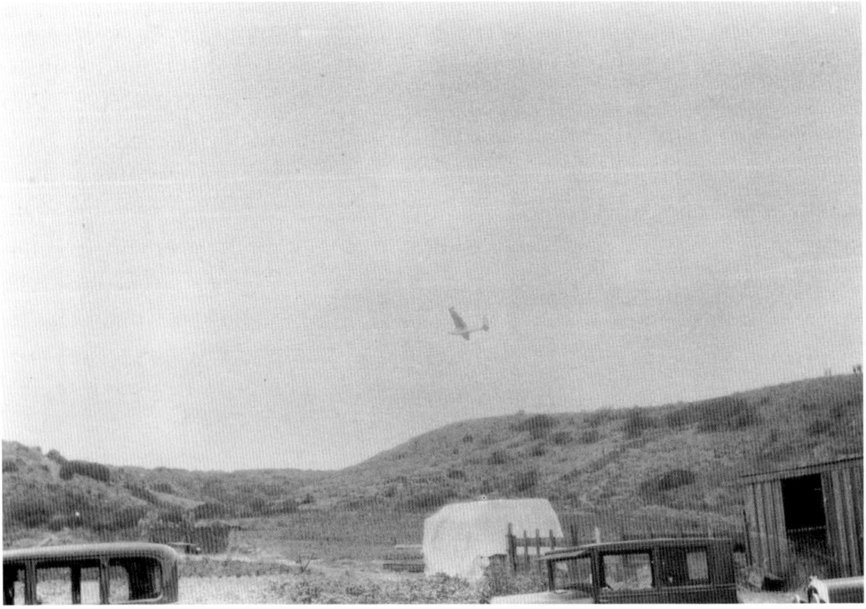

Hawley Bowlus in his SP-1 Paperwing glider soars over Bonita in June 1930. *San Diego Air & Space Museum.*

Vista High School organized a glider club. H. Grafton Chapman, who had retained his interest in gliders even after Shoudy's accident, and Tyce started the first aquatic glider school for Peel Z-1 Glider Boats (more commonly referred to as hydro-gliders), which could be towed on pontoons across the water by a boat and launched into the air, gliding back to a landing on the water. Chapman built a hanger and his first hydro-glider at the Chula Vista Airport. The opening of the school was postponed when testing found the design of the pontoons was not practical. It appears that the entire idea was not practical, as only thirty of the Peel Hydro-Gliders were built before the company went out of business in the Great Depression. Chapman would subsequently work for Consolidated Aircraft, later known as Convair.

POWERED FLIGHT

Unlike other crops, lemons do not benefit from the use of crop dusting, so powered flight remained a rarity in Bonita. However, in May 1930, an unannounced aviation visitor dropped in to the valley. Five Curtis OC-2

Falcon observation airplanes were flying in a V formation at three thousand feet over Bonita when the commander called for them to shift into a single-file formation. Two of the planes crashed into each other and locked up, falling from the sky. All four men on board, two pilots and two observers, were able to parachute to safety. The two pilots, Irvin Masters and Richard DeLacy, were both advanced students on the verge of graduating. One observer, Delroy Anderson, was caught upside down in his plane and had struggled to get his seat belt to release before he could get free and release his parachute. When he landed on Dead Man's Hill, Anderson gathered up his parachute and found pilot DeLacy only one hundred feet away. Anderson was able to render assistance to DeLacy, who was unable to walk at that time and eventually diagnosed with a sprained ankle. Masters was found to have a broken leg, but the other observer, S.G. Davey, was unhurt. The remainder of the squadron flew back to the site and circled low to see if everyone was OK and then returned to base to deliver the news. The audible crash of the planes meant that many folks in Bonita witnessed the accident and the pilots descending with their parachutes. Another explosion, accompanied by a large black cloud, occurred when the planes landed on the mountain. Ambulances and firefighting equipment were sent from Chula Vista, and quite a crowd formed on the hill during the excitement. In October of that year, DeLacy went AWOL after writing some bad checks, and it was thought that he might have incurred a head injury during the crash. He was eventually discharged from the Marines. Military planes continued to fly over the valley, but no others landed in such spectacular fashion.

Sixteen-year-old Larry Weisser, whose family lived on property near the Glen Abbey Cemetery offices, heard the crash and hiked up the mountain to see the wreckage. The Curtiss Falcons were built with aluminum bodies and wooden wings. After the crash and subsequent fire, the Marine Corps removed the debris, but Larry decided to hike back to the crash site the next day. The military had removed the surface debris, but Larry was able to dig up and gather several sizable pieces of aluminum. He and his brothers fabricated hoes and other farm tools from the scrap. Though a real estate dealer by trade, Laurence Weisser Sr. had fallen on hard times, as many did in the 1930s, and the property in Bonita was all the family had left. The three Weisser boys all worked to help the family make mortgage payments on their home through their welding and mechanical experience. Larry later remembered that he gave up the aluminum pieces to a scrap drive during World War II. One such drive was held in March 1942 at the Sweetwater Fruit Company's packing house.

Larry Jr. had moved to the valley when he was young and grew up on his parents' sixty-acre farm. In his younger years, he tended the family's goat herd, which was regularly moved to other properties around the South Bay. Larry delivered newspapers to the valley on horseback while he was attending the F Street School in Chula Vista. After he graduated from high school, Larry drove a school bus in addition to working as a welder. In the years after World War II, Larry and his brothers, Victor and Norman, set up a trucking service. At the same time, using the long stretch of land they owned, they attempted to set up a private airstrip with the owner of Breise Flying School, Fred Breise. (Their property ran along the south side of the present-day Bonita Road, starting at the intersection of Bonita Road and Randy Lane and continuing about a half mile.) In 1946, they graded and leveled the property and installed a wind sock, petitioning the county for a license to operate an airport. They were refused but continued to use the strip for their personal planes. Breise, who had operated out of the La Presa Airport since 1944, moved to Brown Field in 1947. In 1948, neighbors complained again about the airstrip, and Norman Weisser stated that he was flying his personal Vagabond airplane using his own property. Though that was common in the years before the war, in July 1945, San Diego County had enacted an ordinance that required a county permit to construct or operate a runway. The Weisser brothers were told to cease and desist using their property as a landing strip. And the use of the valley for takeoffs and landings came to an end.

5

ELLA BRADFORD COPELAND ALLEN

Dambo and Her Legacy

As someone who grew up in Bonita and went to the Ella B. Allen Elementary School for seven years, I took it for granted that Ella must have been someone of great importance. There are many schools in the area named for superintendents and teachers, so I assumed that's what Ella was. But Ella was a far more interesting person and far more important in the history of Bonita and San Diego. By time that the school board decided to name the first elementary school in Bonita after her, Ella was an old doddering lady with a cane. It's time that people have a clearer picture of Ella Bradford Copeland Allen.

On November 30, 1858, Ella Bradford Copeland was born into a nation on the edge of an enormous upheaval. She was born to a family of privilege and education in Waverley, Massachusetts, where her father, Robert Morris Copeland, and her mother, Josephine Gannett Kent, were both members of prominent families. Morris and Josie (as they were known) were both well educated, he at Harvard and she at the girl's school run by her parents. Josie was one of four daughters of Benjamin Kent—a Unitarian minister before he became a schoolmaster—all of whom taught at the family's school at one time or another. While at Harvard, Morris became friends with Dr. Fredrick Winsor, a friendship that grew after their graduation in 1851 and continued throughout their lives.

By 1854, Morris had established himself in business as a landscape gardener, what we would today refer to as landscape *architect*, with Horace Cleveland. The firm became well known for cemetery designs characterized by creating landscapes that re-created natural settings, something that came into vogue in those years. He also wrote articles both scholarly and popular for many agricultural and landscaping journals as well as daily newspapers. The same year he formed the partnership with Cleveland, Morris married Josephine Kent. Their first son, Frederick, was born in the summer of 1855. And in 1857, the family purchased an eighty-acre farm known as Beaver Brook in Massachusetts. It is here Morris worked on his magnum opus, *Country Life: A Handbook of Agriculture, Horticulture, and Landscape Gardening*, a wide-ranging book of advice for laying out and caring for the grounds of one's estate. The eight-hundred-page tome was a hit, with five editions published in just six years, and it included both practical information as well as Copeland's philosophy of landscaping.

Morris's father and other extended family members had for years owned slate quarries in Vermont. Just after Ella's birth, Morris sold the Beaver Brook property and purchased a property in West Castleton, Vermont, in 1859. The property contained an ongoing slate quarrying concern (Glen Lake Slate Company, primarily for roofing) as well as a steam mill and lumber business that Morris built. The family spent their summers at the Vermont house, where the children had space to roam. Morris worked very hard to make sure his children loved and understood the world around them, especially nature. Ella, in particular, learned a tremendous amount about plants from her father. As Morris stated in *Country Life*,

> *If* [your children] *see your garden arranged for beauty as well as utility, while all over the homestead stern economy occasionally yields to a reverential love of nature and to a sense that gratification of the eye and the mind is quite as important as the gratification of the appetite, they will grow up with liberal, generous feeling and opinions, they will be men and women who have the best interests of the age at heart.*

In early 1861, Morris and a number of like-minded gentlemen of the greater Boston area came together to sign the document that would create the Massachusetts Institute of Technology (MIT). Morris was a close friend of William Barton Rogers, the founder of the school, who had brought these men together. Unfortunately for the signers, within a couple of days, the first shots of the Civil War were fired, leaving the institution to lag until 1865, when the war was over. By that time, Morris had gone on to other concerns and did not continue his professional association with MIT, though his son Frederick attended the school.

The family of four might have settled into an idyllic life had it not been for the outbreak of the Civil War. Because of the family's prominent position, Morris joined a regiment of volunteers. He rose from lieutenant quartermaster to major to serve as assistant adjutant general under Major General Nathaniel Banks, commander of the Second Massachusetts. In November 1861, during a lull in the fighting, Josie brought Frederick and Ella to visit their father in the Shenandoah Valley, where he was stationed with the Second Massachusetts, a visit that Morris fondly referred to in letters home to Josie. Though it may seem odd to our modern sensibilities, many officers were visited at their base camps by their families.

Morris, who was a lifelong abolitionist, was part of the group of men that included Major Robert Gould Shaw, who believed that raising a regiment of free black troops to fight for the Union might win the war sooner. But many in the Union army were not ready to support such a notion, not the least of all President Lincoln. In the spring of 1862, Morris's unit was stationed where a battle against Stonewall Jackson seemed inevitable, and General Banks sent Morris to Washington to plead for reinforcements. Secretly, Morris also planned to push for his plan to create a black regiment. After initially being rebuffed by Secretary of War Edwin Stanton on both fronts, Morris received a telegram from Banks that Jackson was advancing and reinforcements were now crucial. Morris pushed Stanton again, interrupting his dinner, to make his case for more soldiers. He succeeded this time, getting a brigade transferred from Baltimore, and telegraphed that information to Banks.

At this point, Morris's naiveté and lack of understanding of military politics got in his way. After hearing five days later of Jackson's rout of General Banks's forces, Morris wrote a newspaper piece hoping to draw new recruits from Massachusetts, but the stirring prose portrayed the military brass in a less than stellar light and prompted the publishing of editorials critical of the war effort. When Morris finally rejoined his unit, General Banks was taken aback at what he saw as insubordination and suggested Morris apply for a transfer. A few days later, Morris sent a telegram to his brother-in-law Charles Dunbar, who was a newspaperman, about the sorry state of the military as he saw it. Once this communication came to light, Stanton, who was not interested in having a junior officer question his command decisions or military planning, was done with him. Stanton, rather than let Morris be transferred, dismissed him from the service in August 1862, ostensibly for violating trust while serving General Banks.

Morris was thunderstruck by the news of his dismissal. He spent the next few years trying to clear his name, arguing that he deserved a court-martial to hear the charges against him, even writing a pamphlet arguing his case in 1864. Many influential New Englanders, among them Ralph Waldo Emerson, Henry Wadsworth Longfellow and William Barton Rogers, supported his cause, but nothing was to be done with the powers that be in Washington. Separated from his army salary and spending his time trying to clear his name, Morris moved his family into the home of his good friend Frederick Winsor and later to his parents' house. With the war on, few commissions were forthcoming, as people had higher priorities than landscaping their estates.

During Morris's service, Josie and the children had moved back and forth between the Glen Lake house in Vermont and their home in Roxbury. In her letters to Morris, Josie mentions returning to Vermont several times to oversee seasonal work, making it clear that she could handle the family business. Frederick Winsor's wife, Mary Bent (Ware) Winsor, had been a teacher in both public and private schools before they married in 1857. The Winsors moved to Winchester, Massachusetts, in 1864, after Frederick left the U.S. Army. The family built a small house on their property for her to teach school, mostly to her children, but also for other family members and local residents. Frederick and Ella received a good deal of their schooling at Annie's school, making them classmates with Annie's children, including Robert, who was the same age as Ella. The chaos of the years during the Civil War were hard on the Copeland family.

In the years after the Civil War, the Copelands continued to spend time in Vermont, and Morris and Josie welcomed two more sons, William and Robert. The businesses in Vermont began to prosper, adding to the family's income. Morris went back to his landscape work, designing several projects, including the community of Oak Bluffs on Martha's Vineyard and grounds of the Robinson Female Seminary in Exeter, New Hampshire. By the late 1860s, the Copeland family had returned to a normal life, and Morris had regained his prewar position as one of the elite landscape gardeners working in America. Finally, in December 1870, with the change of parties in Washington, Morris was exonerated and given an honorable discharge by President U.S. Grant. The removal of the dark cloud raised the spirits of the entire family as well as the entire community of West Castleton, Vermont.

In 1872, Morris and the family took up residence at Ridley Park. Issac Hinckley, Ridley Park's developer, was hoping to emulate the success of Llewellyn Park by creating a suburb served by his railroad, the Philadelphia,

Wilmington and Baltimore. Morris's design work had begun to include city planning, what we would call master-planned communities, in the late 1860s, and Hinckley hired Morris to create a plan for his subdivision. The trains began service in October 1872, not long after Morris and his family had arrived at Ridley Park. Morris was the first postmaster, appointed on January 9, 1872, and the first justice of the peace.

The Copelands continued to host their relatives often, especially at the home in Vermont. In September 1873, Ella was part of a boating trip on Lake Bomoseen near the family home in Vermont when a squall struck the keel boat and capsized it. The family was hosting the Dunbars at their summer home, Julia Dunbar being Morris's sister, and her husband, Charles Dunbar, a professor at Harvard. Ella's brother Fred, the captain, warned the passengers, which also included his brother James and their cousins Franklin and William Dunbar, to jump free of the boat. Freeing the sail and mast from the boat, they were able to right the craft and, with bailing and rowing, return to shore, though the guns and ammunition were lost. Ella survived the event without a scratch.

In 1873, Morris lost virtually all of his savings as the railroads went through a bust. As Ridley Park was designed to be a railroad suburb, sales were low. Even with low sales, Morris was making $3,000 a year as supervisor and engineer, in addition to any design work he did for other people. Eventually, the project became moderately successful, but Morris would not live to see it. In January 1874, Morris broke his arm in a carriage accident while racing to catch the train. When the injury would not heal, he traveled to Cambridge for a second opinion, and he was diagnosed with cancer. He moved into his sister Julia Dunbar's house and died only two months later in March 1874. Charles Dunbar, who was by then a dean at Harvard, acted as a guardian for Morris and Josie's children, as they had lost a good part of their regular income as well as their savings. Ella later stated that her father showed great fortitude, knowing that his case was terminal and he was leaving his family in financial straits.

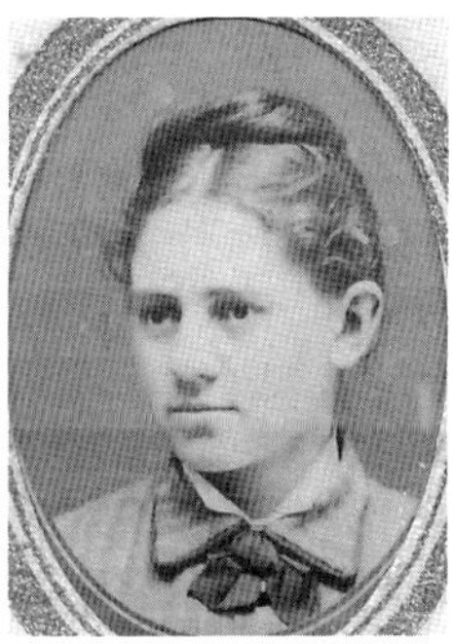

Ella B. Copeland at eighteen years old, two years after her father died. *Allen Mitchum Jr.*

In the wake of Morris's death, Josie and the family returned to the summer home in Vermont, where she ran the farm and the slate quarries as she had done so well during the Civil War. She also began a school and summer camp at her home. With Frederick off at MIT, Ella was the eldest child in the household and assisted her mother with running the school. An advertisement in the *Fair Haven (Vermont) Era* of March 1880 suggests she also taught many botany classes in Massachusetts and she studied at Cambridge. In 1884, Josie moved the family back to Boston, likely to be closer to family. In 1886, Ella prepared to start medical training. She was twenty-seven, unmarried and a girl from a prominent family without much of an inheritance; it's possible she considered this training an appropriate career for an unmarried woman. Instead, her life changed course when she met Russell Allen.

Russell Carpenter Allen was born in Jamaica Plains, Massachusetts, in January 1859, and he spent much of his youth in Cambridge. His father was a minster in the Unitarian Church, though most of his livelihood came from being a teacher of theology and ancient languages rather than a practicing minister. He also did extensive writing and editing on Unitarian theology. Russell was involved in many outdoor activities but especially enjoyed hunting and sailing with his brothers when the family spent summers in Nantucket. The Allen boys—Russell and his brothers, Gardener and Richard—had their own run-in with the sea in Nantucket, where they tipped a boat and it sank. The boys were eventually rescued after swimming several miles.

When Russell was around fourteen, he was hit in the head with a baseball and suffered some damage to his ocular nerve. It took him some months to recover, and for a time, he was schooled at home, since reading was not easy for him. There was concern at one point of a tumor, but after visiting multiple specialists, it was determined that he would just have to go forward with the vision he had in his remaining good eye.

Russell was, even with his vision difficulties, a good student, graduating from Harvard in 1880, with both extended family and celebrities (Theodore Roosevelt) in his graduating class. For a year, he read law in his brother-in-law Charles Gage's office, and though it interested him, the reading was a terrible strain on his eyes, and he knew he would have to find another profession.

In 1881, while his father was a delegate to a Unitarian conference in Transylvania, Russell was able to travel across Europe, where he became intrigued by Mediterranean agriculture when he spent a month in Italy and several weeks in the south of Spain. When he returned from Europe, he decided, therefore, to find an "out-door life & pitched on that of horticulture," though he had previously considered wheat farming or sheep raising. In 1882, he left Cambridge, traveled by boat to Panama, disembarked, crossed the isthmus on foot and embarked on another ship for California.

Warned by his father to avoid wine production because of a prohibition that was rumored to begin soon, in March 1883, he and a partner (George C. Deane) bought land in Dehesa (twenty-five miles southeast of San Diego), partially financed by a gift of capital from Russell's father. The purchase of land was too late in the season for cultivation, and they had to wait a year to set about planting a forty-acre vineyard of raisin grapes and a fifteen-acre orchard of olive trees, both well suited to the dry, rocky climate of the land. Russell found Dehesa to be very like Spain, with similar plants growing amid the dry landscape. He was also a partner with Herbert Dabney in the El Cajon Packing Company. The ranch in Dehesa was isolated and rugged, but there were many opportunities for achievement. Russell's father, mother and sister spent a long portion of the winter of 1884–85 with him at the ranch. Russell's father, Joseph, referred to the land in a letter as "stony hills about, with remote mountains."

Russell returned to Cambridge for Christmas in 1886 and it is there that he "met his fate" in the person of Ella. It was rumored that they met at a party, but there is no doubt that the introduction was made by the Winsors. According to family, they bonded over amateur photography, which Ella had excelled at and which Russell was interested in mastering. Russell and Ella were engaged before he returned to California in the spring of 1887. After the harvest, Russell returned to Cambridge in the winter of 1887, and he and Ella were wed (with his father presiding) in February 1888. They left a week after the wedding for a relaxed three-week journey to Dehesa. To Ella, who had never traveled out of New England, the open countryside and mountainous landscape must have been completely new. Her years with her father had given her a love and understanding of the outdoors, but the dry chaparral countryside must have been quite a shock. Years after, Ella spoke of her fears that the large boulders that dotted the mountainsides would let loose and roll down the hills toward their home.

The ranch in Dehesa had originally been created under Mexican rule, and the family referred to it as Los Paderes. They had intended to name it Los Paredes, for the old adobe wall of the original Mexican land owner, but they misspelled the Spanish word and called it Paderes, which has no meaning. The home was adobe and had been built by Russell the year he arrived, though he added a kitchen annex for his new bride. The property also had a well that served the house and barn. As Russell had hoped,

Ella's love of nature and the outdoor life made her well suited to their life on the ranch.

By 1888, Russell had bought out his partner, and the vines had matured enough to bear good crops, with the firm sending twelve ten-ton carloads of raisins to a Boston firm for sale in 1889. The olive groves also were successful, and Russell and Ella were kept busy curing olives after each growing season. The five-gallon kegs were primarily sent east, though the family kept some. Within a short time, Ella and Russell had three small children with them on the farm: Morris Copeland Allen (1889), Richard Minot Allen (1890) and Eleanor Bradford Allen (1891).

In June 1890, the Sweetwater Fruit Company was formed. Russell was invited, by his cousin Robert Winsor, who had arranged the financing, to become the director of the company. Robert's success at Kidder, Peabody and Company gave him the clout to pull together his business acumen and his family contacts for the new company. On the property that comprised the bulk of the original purchase of land was a house that Henry Cooper built in 1884; the Allen family moved in 1891. This portion of the Sweetwater Valley was not as remote as the property at Dehesa had been, and the home was somewhat larger for the growing family. Around 1894, Ella began educating Morris and Richard at home, calling on her previous experience of teaching alongside her mother. In anticipation of the birth of her next child, Ella sent the boys to the school in Bonita around 1896. Though a year apart in age, they joined the school in the same grade and remained in the same classes for the rest of their schooling.

Under Russell's capable management, the Sweetwater Fruit Company grew and prospered. Though work on the ranch kept him from the famous summer camping trips that Ella planned, he was in high demand to speak about the success of his operation across Southern California. He was involved in the California Fruit Growers Exchange, the San Diego County Fruit Exchange and the Lemon Men's Club, all of which were part of the cooperative marketing that supported the success of citrus growers.

Both Russell and Ella's connections to San Diego grew in these years, even with the long trip by horse and buggy from their home in Bonita to the center of town. In 1896, they became charter members of the College Graduate Club (later the University Club), the group's goal being to bring people together to discuss important topics of the day. It is likely that this is where Ella met Charlotte Baker, San Diego's first female doctor and a New Englander taken by the West Coast. Charlotte and her husband (also a doctor) were very involved in the civic life in San Diego. Dr. Baker was very

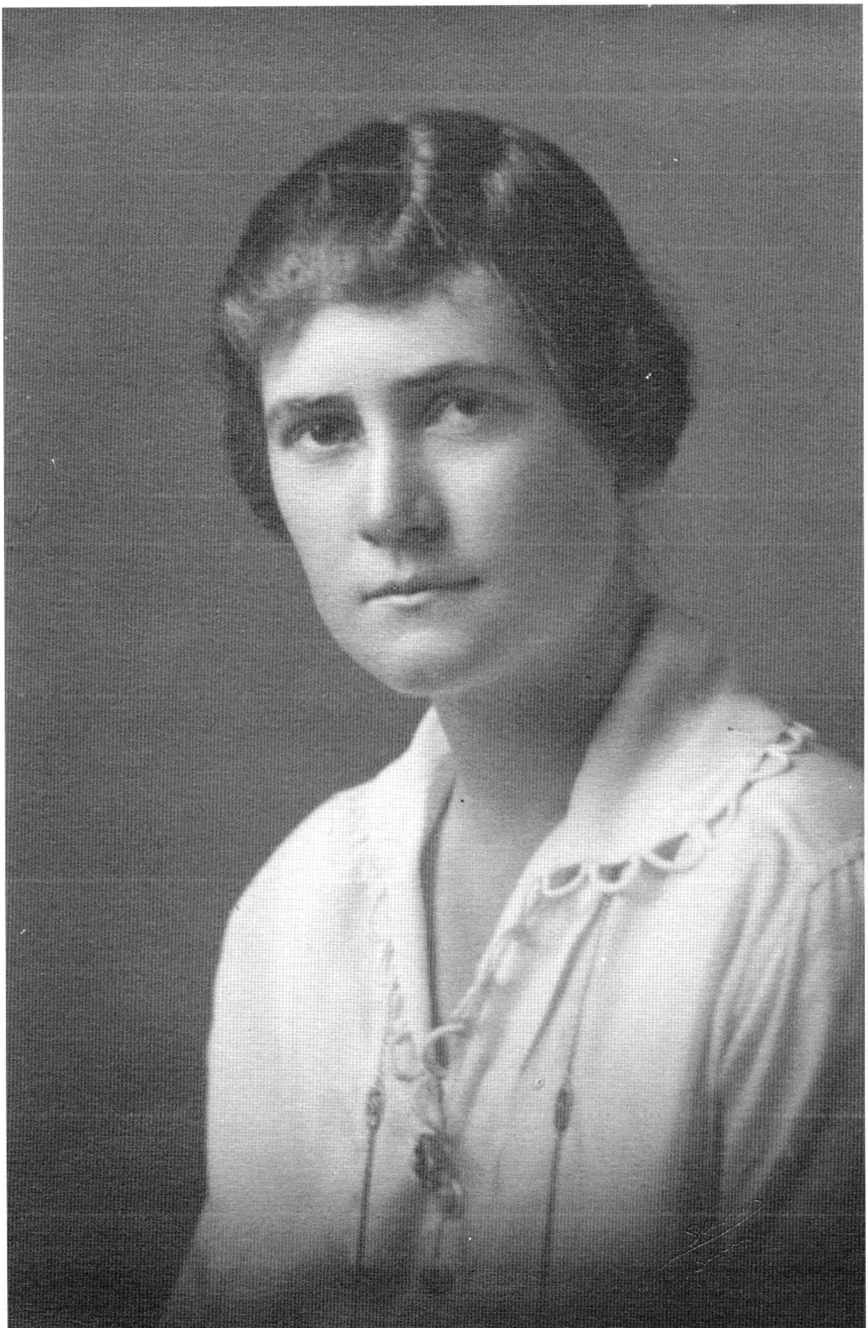

Ella B. Allen in the 1890s. *Allen Mitchum Jr.*

interested in the welfare of women and children, and she worked tirelessly toward that end. She lobbied for an eight-hour day for nurses and advocated for assistance for women with children in addition to founding the San Diego YWCA. She delivered over one thousand babies and prided herself on the fact she never lost a mother. Ella and Charlotte became good friends, though to hear her children tell it, almost everyone Ella met became her friend.

In April 1897, Mary Ware Allen was born, with Ella attended by her good friend Charlotte Baker. In November of that year, Russell, Ella and Mary survived what must have been a harrowing accident. Driving down the grade from the Sweetwater Dam, the horse ran over the embankment. Russell and Ella attempted to jump, but Ella was hampered by holding Mary and couldn't get out in time. She rode the wagon down the steep embankment, and though Mary was fine, Ella did suffer a badly broken ankle, which was never properly set. Russell had jumped clear and was fine, going to a nearby house for help. The wagon was not as lucky and was "reduced to kindling wood."

The turn of the century was relatively quiet for the Allen family. Ella's mother, Josie, had moved from Boston to Bonita. The ten years that Ella had been in California were the longest she and her mother had lived apart, and she was very pleased to have her mother close by. In addition to successfully running the citrus ranch, the Allens continued to grow raisins and olives on the ranch in Dehesa. There were family trips to the beaches of La Jolla and the Tent City on Coronado.

Russell spent the summer months of 1902 on a commission evaluating locations to relocate the Cupeño Indians. By a U.S. Supreme Court decision, the Cupeño were being forced to move from their ancestral grounds on the Warner Ranch. The chosen location was widely protested, and the government allowed the creation of a commission to find a more suitable place, with a $2,500 stipend to defray the costs of the endeavor. Charles F. Lummis, a classmate of Russell's at Harvard who had dropped out, nominated him to be part of the commission, which had ninety days to finish inspections and submit a report. The commission, consisting of Allen, Lummis and Charles L. Partridge and their team, was required to visit each offered piece of land and submit a detailed report on each, including the size, availability of water, any existing crops or improvements and suitable locations for housing and future crops.

The group, which included a local civil engineer, a photographer, a stenographer and Lummis's daughter Turbesé, left in early July. The commission undertook two trips and traveled hundreds of miles by train, horseback and on foot to evaluate forty offers of land encompassing over 150,000 acres into the backcountry of San Diego County, all without any personal compensation. The expedition used a four-mule freight wagon with a chuck wagon kitchen set up, a driver, a cook and 2,800 pounds of supplies. Many landowners coveted the $100,000 that the U.S. government was willing to spend on a new home for the Cupeño. The commission finally decided on the Pala tract in the San Luis Rey Valley, encompassing over 3,000 acres. Though in retrospect the decision seems quite heavy-handed, at the time it was considered a win-win for the Cupeño.

Through his connections on the commission, especially Charles Lummis, Russell was introduced to Frank Mead, an architect who had been involved in an attempt to assist the Yavapai with their historic tribal land in Arizona since 1901. Mead continued working in Arizona with the Bureau of Indian Affairs for the next three years. This chance meeting would prove to be important for both men.

In 1903, Mary went off to school, giving Ella more free time to participate in efforts outside of the home. We know that Russell and Ella were both what today are labeled *civic-minded* individuals. We do not know how early Ella was involved in the suffrage movement, but we know that by 1905, she was a member of and the corresponding secretary for the San Diego Equal Suffrage Association (which organized in 1904). As someone so involved in civic affairs, it must have galled Ella that she had no actual say in which people were elected to govern locally and nationally. Ella and Charlotte Baker's friendship intensified while they both worked to get women the vote.

In August 1906 a small tragedy befell the Allen family. The original house built by Henry Cooper burned down, possibly started by an oil lamp. Nobody was injured, but the house was a total loss, though the workers living in the nearly bunkhouse where able to run into the structure and retrieve some furniture and personal items. The family took over a portion of the packing house to live in, having their cooking and living space in the adobe portion and their sleeping quarters in the wooden potion. They utilized canvas dividers, usually used for storing the lemons for curing, as walls. They had a stove for heating purposes and food preparation. Russell was all for renting a home in National City during this period, but Ella was interested in overseeing the construction of her new home.

Once the family had living arrangements, it was time to find an architect for their new home. We don't know if Frank Mead offered his services or if Russell sought him out, but knowing Mead made it an easy choice. Because of the fire scare, the Allens wanted a home that would be very hard

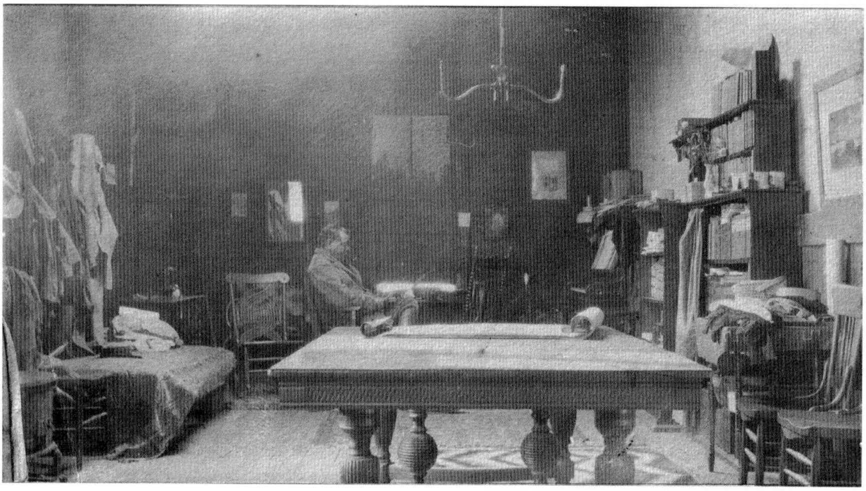

Above: Russell C. Allen in the temporary residence set up in the packing house after the Allen house burned down in 1906. *California Genealogical Society, Manuscript Collection.*

Opposite, top: Eleanor Allen in the temporary living room space in the packing house. *California Genealogical Society, Manuscript Collection.*

Opposite, bottom: Sleeping and bathing quarters set up in the wooden storage shed portion of the packing house. *California Genealogical Society, Manuscript Collection.*

to burn down, and Mead and Irving Gill used new construction methods with concrete and hollow tile on the new structure. Though the house was designed during Mead and Gill's short partnership, it is significant that Mead completed the construction on his own, acting as general contractor. From the time of the fire in 1906 until March 1908, Ella and her family not only ran the Sweetwater Fruit Company, they lived in it as well.

Late in 1906, Josie Copeland began to falter. It is possible that she had a stroke, and on June 14, 1907, Josie died. She was cremated, and her ashes were returned to Massachusetts to be buried next to her husband, Morris. She and Ella had been companions for a good portion of her adult life. The joy over Morris and Richard graduating from the Thatcher School and preparing to go off to Harvard had to have been tempered by the loss of their grandmother.

Ella had been planning a trip into Baja California to "do something a little out of the ordinary before the boys left the home roost." This is not the first camping trip that Ella had planned, as the family had camped all over Baja California in prior summers, Ella often including her children's

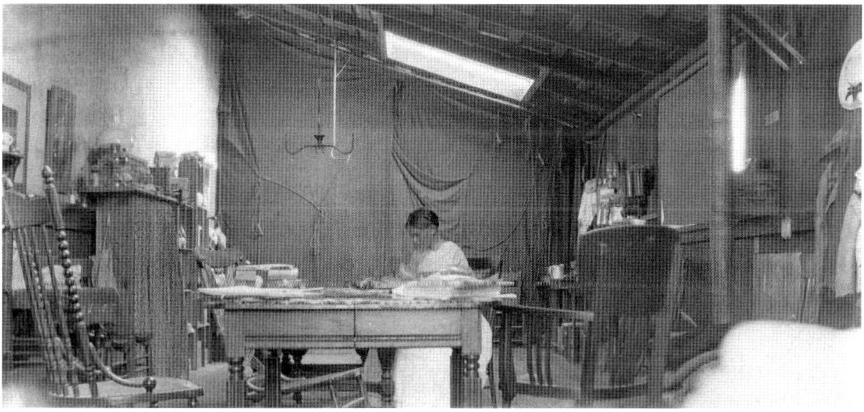

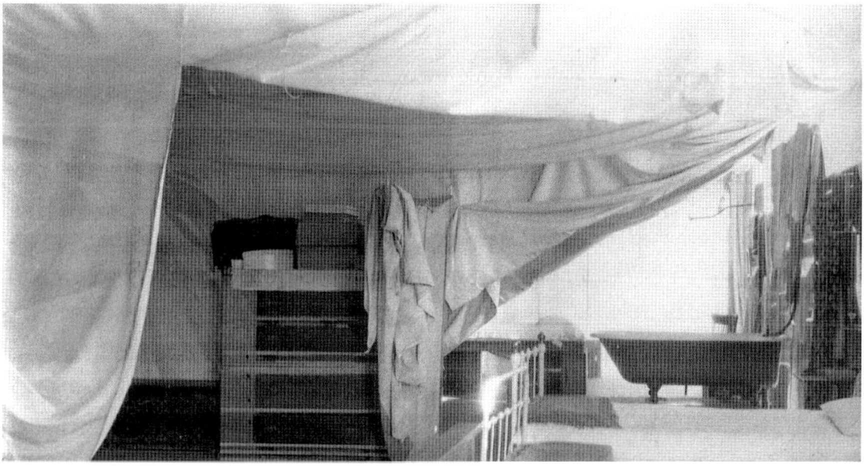

friends as well. But their trip to San Pedro de Mártir Mountain would be a grand adventure that the children and Ella would speak of for years to come. Mary, by virtue of her young age, and Russell, because of the busy summer season in the orchards, would not be able to go.

Known today as Sierra de San Pedro Mártir National Park in Ensenada, the park is home to the largest optical telescope in Mexico, and the tallest peak is over ten thousand feet. First explored by the Jesuits, it was later home to the Mission de San Pedro Mártir de Verona, built by the Dominicans in 1794. They abandoned the mission by the 1820s because of its remote location. Even today, visiting the site requires going into the mountains by foot.

Ella kept a journal of the trip and later wrote up an account titled "A Trip to San Pedro Mártyr Mountain." The group consisted of Morris, Richard and their friend Charlie Nordoff; Eleanor and her friend Julia Kommers; and Ella. They rode the steamer *St. Denis* to San Quentín and met up with their guide, Captain E.W. Funcke, and his assistant Salvador Mesa, who would assist with the animals and other jobs during the trip. They had five burros, three mules and a small black horse. The burros were used primarily as pack animals, the mules for supplies and riding and the black horse for riding. Between the six travelers, there were two animals to ride at a time while the other four would walk.

Ella was not just along for the ride on this trip. She did most of the cooking and commented that by the end of the trip, she had been "smoke-cured." (The loss of the stove pipe on the fourth day did nothing to make that better.) They carried mostly dry supplies with the exception of canned milk, and they supplemented their menu with fish and deer caught along the trail. Ella captured grasshoppers for Morris to use as bait for fishing, removing their heads in the process. They brought few comforts of home, although Ella recounted reading both *Guy Mannering* and *David Copperfield* in the evenings by the campfire, so she did carry a few books with her. Ella also carried a drawstring bag with her on the trip and picked up seeds from all the various plants she saw, many of which would end up planted in her garden.

The bulk of her account of the trip involves describing the scenery along their route, including the topography of rivers and her guesses of the geology of the mountains. She also described in great detail the people they met along the way, including those with whom they stayed and others they passed along the mountains. Ella bemoaned not speaking better Spanish because it put her at a disadvantage when trying to communicate with the people they met along the trail. Of particular interest is a man that she mentioned meeting at least twice, a Mr. North. Arthur Walbridge North was traveling in Baja California and, in 1910, published *Camp and Camino in Lower California*, a record of his several months along peninsular California. While his account does not mention them by name, North does mention that "we found camped at Vallecitos a plucky American woman, surrounded by her boys and girls." Based on Ella's journal, her group was camped at Vallacitos the second time they encountered Mr. North. And Ella certainly was plucky!

Ella's remembrance of the trip also includes lost people, stubborn burros, hot weather, cold rain, blisters and assorted scrapes, bumps and bruises to all members of the party. The highlight of the trip for all involved was arriving high enough on San Pedro Mártir to look across and see the desert and on to the gulf on the eastern side of the peninsula. Ella

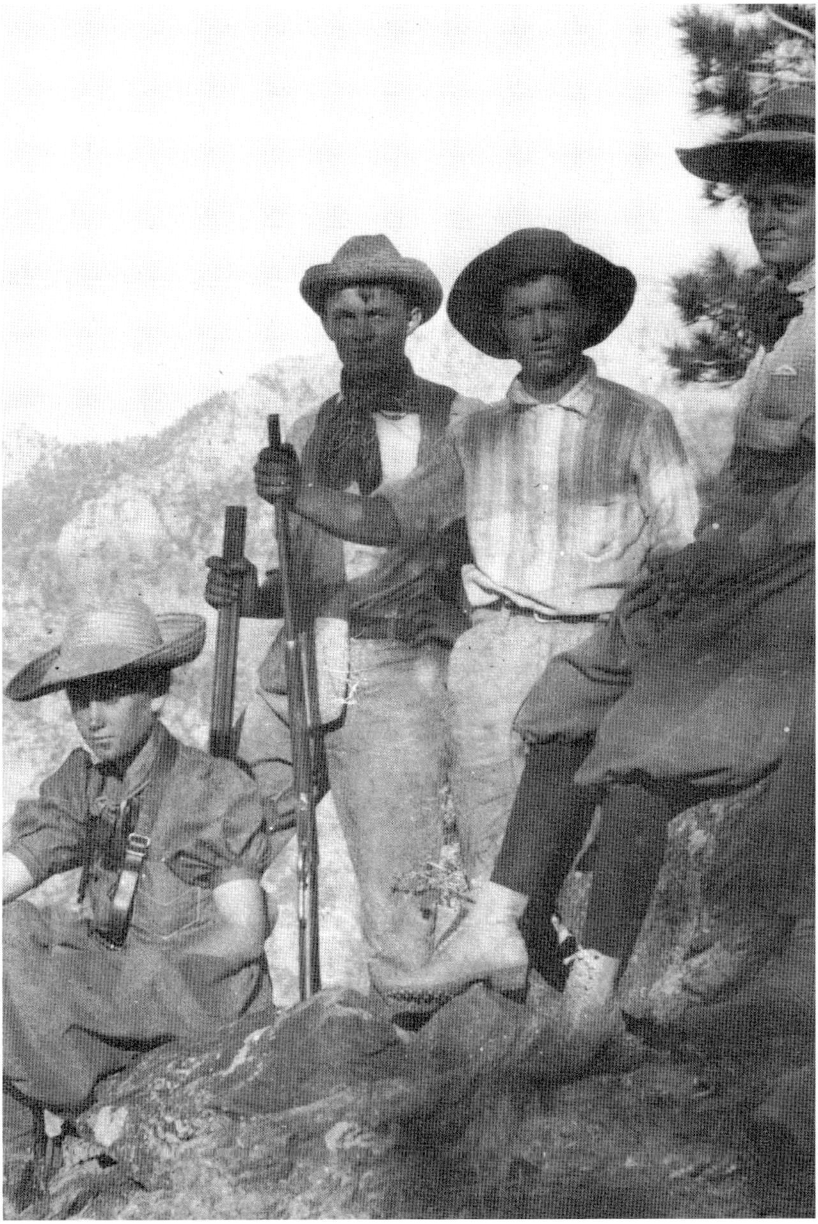

Left to right: Eleanor B. Allen, Charlie Nordoff, Morris C. Allen and Julia Kommers on the trip to San Pedro de Mártyr in 1906. *California Genealogical Society, Manuscript Collection.*

made several trips to the skyline, one that coincided with sunset and made for a tricky descent in the dark. Later, Ella opined that "the views from the Eastern sky line [*sic*] we knew we should never see equaled until we came back to the same spot again, which we should probably never do except in imagination." There's a sadness in this that seems very clear in the light of her mother's death only a few weeks before.

Ella's remembrance of the trip is one of the few things we have written in her own hand, and it shows her to be constantly amazed by the world around her, humbled by the kindness of people and full of joy for the experience she and the children were able to share. She spoke highly of the Mexicans she encountered and contradicted the opinions of contemporaries who complained that they were lazy or unmotivated. And though she made the trip in skirts and buttoned shoes, Ella never complained about the conditions on the trail. The entire group had quite an adventure, and Morris and Richard went off to Harvard with many stories to tell.

Though the Allen family had been out of their house for over a year, it is not until the fall of 1907 that plans were drawn up for their new home. There may have been previous plans that fell through, but considering the speed at which their new house was completed, there must have been some issue that has been lost to time. Irving Gill and Frank Mead began their partnership in May 1907 and designed only three buildings before the partnership dissolved in November. Frank Mead and Russell Allen had been most taken by visits to the Alhambra in Spain and enjoyed the architecture of southern Spain and Morocco. There are strong influences of this architecture and the Puebloan architecture that Mead spent the previous years working among in the design of the Allens' new home. Ella also had definite ideas about what her new home should include, especially a large central space for holding parties.

Construction on the house commenced after the drawings were completed on November 16. Russell drove to Chula Vista and brought Frank Mead and his friend George Curtis out to the valley to see the construction on November 26. Mead and Curtis joined the Allens for Thanksgiving dinner, where discussion of Russell's work with the Cupeño and Mead's work with the Yavapai would've been a likely conversation. The end of the Gill and Mead partnership may have also been discussed. (Curtis was interested in running a ranch and spent several weeks in early 1907 working for the Sweetwater Fruit Company.) The promise of spring in 1908 also included the promise of living in their new home. As much as Ella enjoyed camping, she was happy to have a roof over her head that she didn't have to share

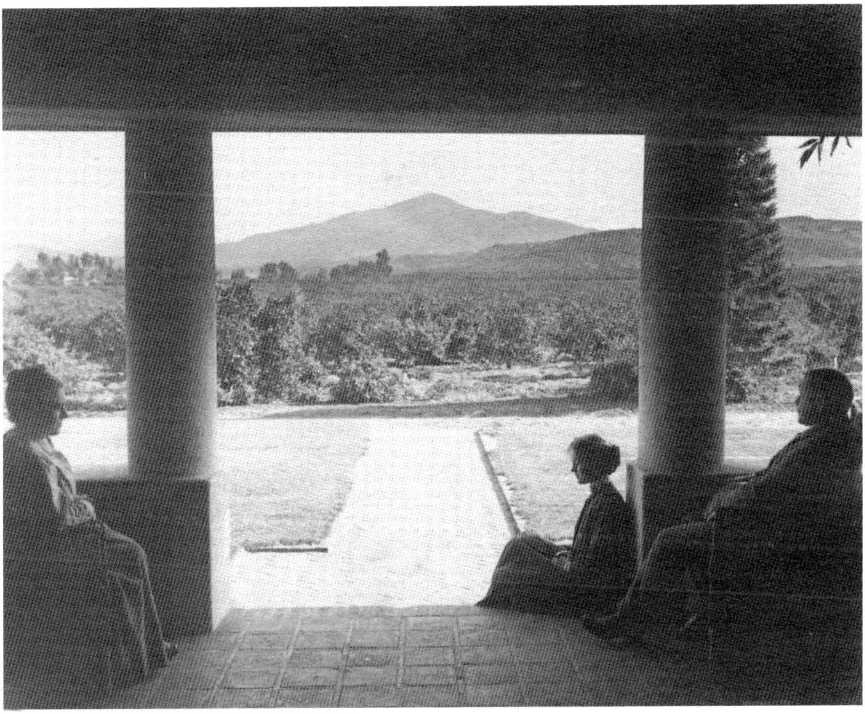

A photo taken in the covered entryway of the Gill and Mead–designed house, with San Miguel Mountain framed in the archway behind a sea of lemon trees. *Left to right*: Ella, Eleanor and Russell Allen. *Allen Mitchum Jr.*

with boxes of lemons. The Allens hosted Mead and Curtis again on March 17 for a celebratory dinner in their new home. The completion of the house allowed Ella to turn her attention to work on the garden, including planting many of the seeds she gathered on her trip to Baja California.

Ella never stopped participating in the civic life of Bonita and San Diego, and in 1909, her husband, Russell, became the president of the University Club, which entailed many duties for Ella, planning and assisting in the various events that the club held. It is at around this time that Ella turned her full efforts to being what some would call a civic matriarch, using her free time to oversee the well-being of her community rather than her family.

According to everyone who knew her, as much as Ella enjoyed her efforts around the community, she also loved hosting and attending parties. The new Allen home had been designed with a large central space that could be cleared to hold events, and if the Allen home wasn't large enough, Ella would take over the packing house. (The packing house's hardwood floors were considered quite good for dancing.) She taught her children to include everyone during these events, requiring the boys to make sure everyone had a dance partner. In 1909, she wrote a letter to the paper complaining that the National City schools were prohibiting dancing. She understood that students should work hard at their studies but asserted that they should also have the chance on Friday and Saturday nights for wholesome activities and relaxation. She also found that in a region that couldn't support boating or skating or sledding, dancing offered exercise and interaction. The kids who grew up in the valley spent many a fun evening at packing house parties hosted by Ella. She was known to play the piano at these events, though her repertoire was limited to three or four songs. And she with the other mothers often ended the evenings by driving the children to their homes before returning to her home, putting up the horse for the night and maybe setting her bread before going off to bed. Ella's daughter Mary said that "good time for young folks was her creed!"

The Allens still owned their property in Dehesa and continued to grow olives. Ella sent casks of olives to Morris, Richard and Eleanor while they were off at college, making the Allen children's rooms a favorite place to study. The cultivation of raisins stopped in the 1910s, as Fresno became the region for California raisin crops.

In 1910, Russell was appointed to the Building and Grounds Committee of the Panama-California Exposition. The expo, which joined the Panama-Pacific International Exposition in San Francisco, celebrated the opening of the Panama Canal and was intended to market San Diego as the first U.S. port north of Panama. For Russell, who traversed the Isthmus of Panama on his journey to San Diego, participating in the celebration must have had special meaning. Creating such a signature event for San Diego was important to civic pride. In 1910, Eleanor went off to college at Bryn Mawr. Though Ella had taken college classes, she never had the opportunity to complete a degree, and she was adamant that her daughters would go to college. Mary also attended Bryn Mawr but decided after a year it was too East Coast for her, and she eventually received her degree from Berkeley.

The entries in Charlotte Baker's diaries indicate that she had continued to work for the Equal Suffrage Association since the first vote in 1896, but there had been little progress. However, in 1910, control of the state legislature passed to the Progressives, who, under newly elected governor Hiram Johnson, submitted twenty-three amendments, including one that would call for a special election in October 1911 to vote on suffrage for women. Southern California had overwhelmingly approved of suffrage in the 1896 vote, but that effort was defeated in Northern California. Charlotte and Ella, who was elected corresponding secretary again for the Equal Suffrage Association in 1911, knew that their organization needed to work to increase their margins. The bill to allow the vote was approved in early February, and the supporters had to hit the ground running, with only eight months to prepare. Charlotte and Ella spearheaded the campaign in San Diego, which included billboards, speakers and printed materials of all types. Dividing the city into precincts, they assigned a leader or "captainess," who oversaw canvassing homes in her district.

The committee in charge of the Panama-California Exposition organized a parade for July 22, 1911, to celebrate the groundbreaking for the expo, part of a day of general celebration for the city. The Equal Suffrage Association submitted an application to participate in the parade. The float, drawn by six horses, was titled "The Modern Boston Tea Party" and was in the shape of a sailing ship with yellow sails (yellow being the color adopted by the suffrage movement). It included the slogan "Taxation Without Representation Is Tyranny Now as It Was in 1773." Ella's children and their friends were the passengers on the float, dressed as Indians. (The only reason I have found for the Indian costumes was that some of the original Boston Tea Party protestors were dressed as such.)

There was organized opposition to the Equal Suffrage Association from the Southern California Association Opposed to Women's Suffrage, and another organization, Committee of Fifty Opposed to the Adoption of Constitutional Amendment No. 8, that started up in the months before the vote was to take place. The conservative and influential businessmen made arguments against women's suffrage, including that the votes of intelligent women would be offset by the votes of ignorant women or that the stress of choosing who to vote for would be too much for women's psychological well-being. In Northern California, saloon owners opposed women's suffrage because they believed it would lead to greater power for temperance, which was more widely supported by women.

As the October date neared, Charlotte, Ella, Ella's daughter Eleanor, Lydia Harris and Mrs. George Norton set out on an auto trip to the back country of San Diego in a decorated car. (Eleanor and Lydia went as the drivers; though Ella had been taught to drive a car, she "simply could not seem to learn to drive a car herself.") On September 4, they traveled from downtown San Diego to Oceanside, where they handed out literature and spoke on benches while onlookers ate their lunches, and went on to

Escondido in the evening. The next day, they drove to Fallbrook, where they had a hard time finding the correct road but eventually had a great audience. They continued on to Ramona, where they spoke at the town hall before returning home the next day. The use of a car as a platform for speaking was done by many women during the fight for suffrage as they didn't need to find or rent a stage from which to speak. Charlotte later wrote that Ella was her "right hand woman" in the fight for suffrage, essential to the success of the venture, and the two continued "auto speaking," as Charlotte called it, for the next month to advance their cause.

On the day of the election, Charlotte and Ella stayed at headquarters until two o'clock in the morning awaiting the result. As it happened in the 1896 election, suffrage carried in San Diego County. The wait was to see whether the votes from Northern California would come out against women's suffrage. It took three days for the complete tabulation of the votes, and in the end, it was a very close race. The measure passed by a margin of 3,500 votes in total, an average of one vote in each precinct in the state. After the results were known, Dr. Baker received a phone call from the city clerk informing her that she could register to vote, which she promptly did. She and three other women were sworn in as deputies so they could set about registering other women, and it is very likely that Ella registered at the same time. The Equal Suffrage Organization continued its work through registering women and helping them understand their duties as voters. Ella was quoted in the paper: "I represent the third generation of workers for, and believers in, equal suffrage, and I wish my mother and grandmother were here to hear the news." The organization also hosted a "grand jollification" of their victory at the YWCA, preceded by an information session about the upcoming vote on harbor bonds, the first issue on which members would be able to vote.

In March 1911, a group of women living in the Sweetwater Valley decided the local community needed some place to gather and started to collect money for a clubhouse. On March 23, Ella and twenty-six other women chartered the Sweetwater Woman's Club as a "neighborly social hour." The original dues were twenty-five cents a year, and meetings were held in members' houses. By 1913, the women had built a small clubhouse, where they held events for themselves and the community. The year 1911 was a busy one for the Allen family, as both Morris and Richard graduated from Harvard in the spring. Richard went to work with his father at the Sweetwater Fruit Company, and Morris took over managing the ranch at Dehesa.

With the impending Panama-California Exposition in 1916, local city leaders were interested in removing the unsavory element from the area just south of Broadway in downtown. The Progressives who brought in women's suffrage also brought other improvements to society—trash pickup, building codes and crackdowns on vice. With the fight for suffrage behind them, Ella and Charlotte were interested in working on the project of cleaning up in the Stingaree (what is today known as the Gaslamp District in San Diego). The Stingaree was a collection of buildings home to saloons, gambling halls, houses of prostitution, San Diego's first Chinatown and lodging for the destitute. Both Ella and Charlotte were of the opinion that it was women and children who suffered most in an area like the Stingaree, considering them "more sinned against than sinner." Dr. Baker, in particular, fought against vice for medical reasons—tuberculosis and venereal disease being rampant in such districts.

They worked with the YWCA and the Purity Union to try to bring services to the women in hopes that they would leave behind lives of prostitution. In 1897, a group of women started the Door of Hope, and they opened a "rescue home for fallen women" at 1243 Front Street in downtown. In 1912, the renewed effort to clean up the area brought the Door of Hope back to prominence, and it officially incorporated as the Door of Hope Association. As early as that year, the City of San Diego appropriated money to the organization for its work. Charlotte and Ella had made a study of the conditions in Los Angeles and were concerned with ascertaining the best way to take care of the women who would be driven from the district, and they submitted a report to the superintendent of the San Diego police. It stated that their organization was ready to provide support for such women the police deemed "worthy of assistance," which was a condition the San Diego police required before they would clear the district.

City leaders, however, thought that the best way to make the problem go away was to round up the women and give them a one-way ticket on a train out of town. With the local health officer closing and condemning buildings and women evicted and run out of town, there were some permanent changes in the Stingaree. (Many of the condemned buildings had held opium dens and other businesses owned by Chinese immigrants, and their destruction forced many of those citizens into homelessness.) It's impossible to know how many women turned around and came back to town and found other locations to work. Using the health officer to close and destroy some of the worst of the buildings in the Stingaree did change the neighborhood, and by 1915, the Stingaree was not quite the red-light district that it had been only a few years before.

The Door of Hope operated in two locations in 1911 and 1912, but it was soon having to turn away potential clients and looked toward building a new home. Funds to erect a new building for the Door of Hope were being solicited to create a new site for women to go to, and the organization brokered a deal with the City of San Diego for lease on land within Collier Park. Collier had been a developer in Ocean Beach and had given a large plot to the city of land as a public park. As part of the Door of Hope's lease, at such time as it ended the lease, the building would become the property of the City of San Diego.

Mary Ward remembered that it was her mother, Ella, who brought Frank Mead and Richard Requa to the project in the kind but heavy-handed way that she had, and she worked tirelessly to raise the funds for the structure. The building, located at 2301 Bolinas Street, was two stories surrounding a small courtyard, including twenty rooms and a complete birthing facility. It also included a separate section for nurse and other worker housing to give the workers a measure of privacy. The facility served San Diego until 1962, when a new building was completed. The structure on Bolinas Street, which reverted to the City of San Diego after the Door of Hope ended its lease, was abandoned and sat boarded up for over a decade before it was demolished and replaced by an apartment complex.

Late in 1912, Ella's maiden aunt Isabel Kent came to live with the Allens in Bonita. Isabel was one of Josie's two sisters who had never married. Eloisa and Isabel had both been teachers at the Kent's School for Girls and lived together in Massachusetts all of their lives, both with other family and on their own. Isabel was in her eighties and not in the best of health when Ella began to care for her.

The prominent women of San Diego repeatedly asked the Panama-California Exposition Board to allot them space and responsibilities within the expo, as had been done in the previous World's Fairs in Chicago and St. Louis. The board stonewalled for many years, apparently fearing that the women would require that no alcohol sales be permitted at the event. When the board eventually acquiesced in June 1914, it was too late for the women to have their own building, but they were offered a large space as well as money for certain cultural exhibits. Their space included a room for dignitaries, restrooms and a day nursery, a first for any fair up to that time. All of the wives of the board members were made ex-official members of the Woman's Committee, making Ella part of the group. In support of her husband, it's evident that Ella stayed out of the fray, but it's clear she was on the side of the women fighting for their representation. Ella was also active in supporting George Marston for mayor of San Diego in both of his runs—1913 and 1917—and involved her entire family in supporting his cause of "geraniums versus smokestacks," a concept that was quite dear to her heart.

It is around this time that Ella B. Allen started to be known as Dambo, especially to her grandchildren. It was probably one of those names that was a misstatement of "grandma," but no one knows. (Dambo is the word for shallow wetlands in an African language, but it appears to have no connection.) But for her grandchildren, and many others, Ella was Dambo for the rest of her life.

In 1915, Ella took on the presidency of the Boys and Girls Aid Society. This organization was begun to meet the needs of children who were not being helped by the local Women's and Children's Home. Mary Ward noted that the organization had a hand-to-mouth existence even with the work that her mother and many other people put into it. It was yet another place that Ella directed her efforts to help women and children have better lives.

In January 1916, a series of storms brought a tremendous amount of rain the San Diego, rain that caused flooding across the county and damage to property and loss of life. The Otay Dam was washed away, and the Sweetwater Dam suffered damage. Water covered the valley from side to side, and many objects were washed to the sea, including railcars. Automobile owners were forced to put chains on their tires for traction navigating the dirt roads in the valley. Months were spent clearing and repairing farms and fields on the valley floor. Morris, after cleaning up flood debris at the family's properties in Dehesa and Bonita, went to work running Robert Winsor's ranch. Winsor's ranch eventually included a dairy and a hog-raising business. The Sweetwater Woman's Club clubhouse was lost in the flood, washed away with its contents, including a brand-new player piano, kitchen equipment, chairs, a stage and a library.

Ella's life in the 1910s was mightily improved by the addition of a Ford Model T. This setup, with a hand-operated throttle and a simplified pedal system, allowed Ella to finally master the art of driving. The new Model T pickup truck allowed Ella to carry children, plants and equipment or just about anything she wanted anywhere she wanted. She was known for whizzing around the dirt roads in the Sweetwater Valley at maybe not quite the speed limit. She had the occasional run-in with a fire hydrant or

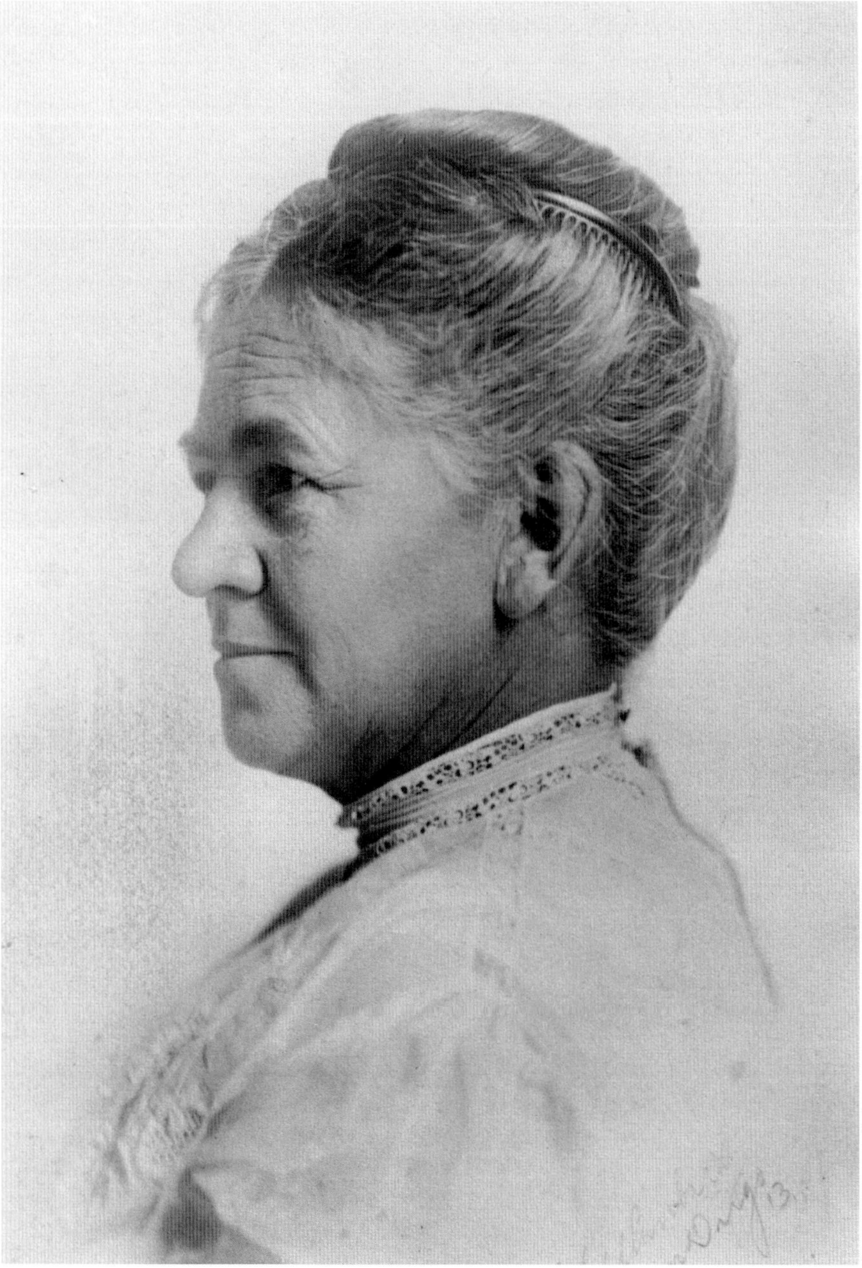

Ella B. Allen around 1913. *Allen Mitchum Jr.*

a fence—and once with a man on a bicycle, though he was not hurt. For a woman who was born long before cars became a reality, the ease of driving herself anywhere she wanted, without having to hitch and unhitch horses and buggy, had to have been quite a convenience.

When the United States entered World War I in April 1917, Russell became the chair of the draft board, and Morris's number was one of the first called. Though he had a dependent family, because his father agreed to provide for Morris's wife and children, Morris was able to be one of, if not the first, man from San Diego inducted. Between training, assignments in the United States and a bout with influenza, Morris didn't arrive at the lines in France until November 4, 1918, just a week before the armistice. He finally made it home in March 1919. During his absence, Ella had kept busy with the other members of the Sweetwater Woman's Club, which had suspended its traditional activities and became a Red Cross Auxiliary, meeting in members' homes to roll bandages and knit socks and mufflers for the soldiers.

During the 1920s, Ella continued to stay busy. Her newest project was Casa de Salud, which grew out of concerns about the high mortality of children born in National City. The program began as a weekly medical clinic for babies, run with assistance from the Community Chest. From a small space on Seventh Avenue in National City, the outreach expanded to baby clinics and parenting classes, arts and crafts classes and citizenship classes, and during the Great Depression, it fed upward of forty-eight children a day. In addition to Ella's ongoing support, the Sweetwater Woman's Club give one of its famed community barn dances to support Casa del Salud in 1931.

Ella again served as the president of the Boys and Girls Aid Society of San Diego. She served on the state GOP committee. She regularly called and raised money for the local Community Chest. When the local students moved out of the one-room Bonita schoolhouse in 1922, the Sweetwater Woman's Club moved in and began hosting events there. That year, Ella served as the president, overseeing all sorts of social events, including dances, dramatic entertainments, card parties and community dinners. The club continued to offer programs, hold the yearly bazaar and raise money in hopes of once again having a clubhouse.

In June 1927, Ella's beloved husband, Russell, died. He had been ill for a few weeks before his death, but up to that point, he had been in such good health that it came as a shock to everyone. He had recently completed a trip to the east and returned by way of the Panama Canal this time rather than overland. Accolades and honors poured in from around the country, including a tribute by George Marston that was published in the *San Diego Union*. Russell's well-attended funeral was held at his home in Bonita, and though mourners were asked not to send flowers, the house was festooned with blossoms from Ella's garden. Richard, who had been working with his father since the 1910s, took over as the head of the Sweetwater Fruit Company.

Russell had created a trust for his assets to provide for Ella for the rest of her life. With all of her children grown and out of the house, Ella decided to move across the valley to a smaller house and sell the lovely Mead and Gill home she had lived in for nearly twenty years. Moving did not slow her down in the least, and she continued to host fundraisers and be involved in civic activities all over Bonita and San Diego.

In October 1932, Ella was involved in an auto accident that reinjured the ankle she had broken so many years before. Her car hit Mrs. Chapman's car on a blind corner in Bonita. Though it was initially reported that her condition was not serious, in reality, the injury to her ankle kept her in Elwyn Sanitarium in National City for several weeks, and there was talk that she might never be able to walk again. She finally returned home ten weeks later, though she still had trouble getting around. A year later, the newspaper reported that she recovered sufficiently to walk about her house and grounds with a cane. The newspaper gave her motto as "never give up." According to her children, this injury forced Ella to use a wheelchair most of the time, but she was not defined by being an invalid, though she did have live-in help from this time forward. In the winter of 1933–34, Ella took an extended visit to see Morris, who was then living and working in Texas with his wife and children. She continued to get around to see friends and attend events, and she still worked the phone to raise money for Community Chest and other special events.

In 1933, the Sweetwater Fruit Company (likely with some light arm-twisting from Ella) donated a parcel of land slightly above the river in a lovely grove of eucalyptus trees to the Woman's Club. In 1934, Vi Horton engaged in the services of Cliff May to design a new clubhouse, and after years of fundraising, on June 30, 1934, the club held its opening event in the eucalyptus grove. The structure had an open-beamed meeting space with a fireplace as well as a kitchen and patio. At that event in 1934, Ella made a presentation called "The History of Bonita," possibly the first time anyone had actually compiled the history of the little community. She was well suited for the task, as she had lived there for over forty years.

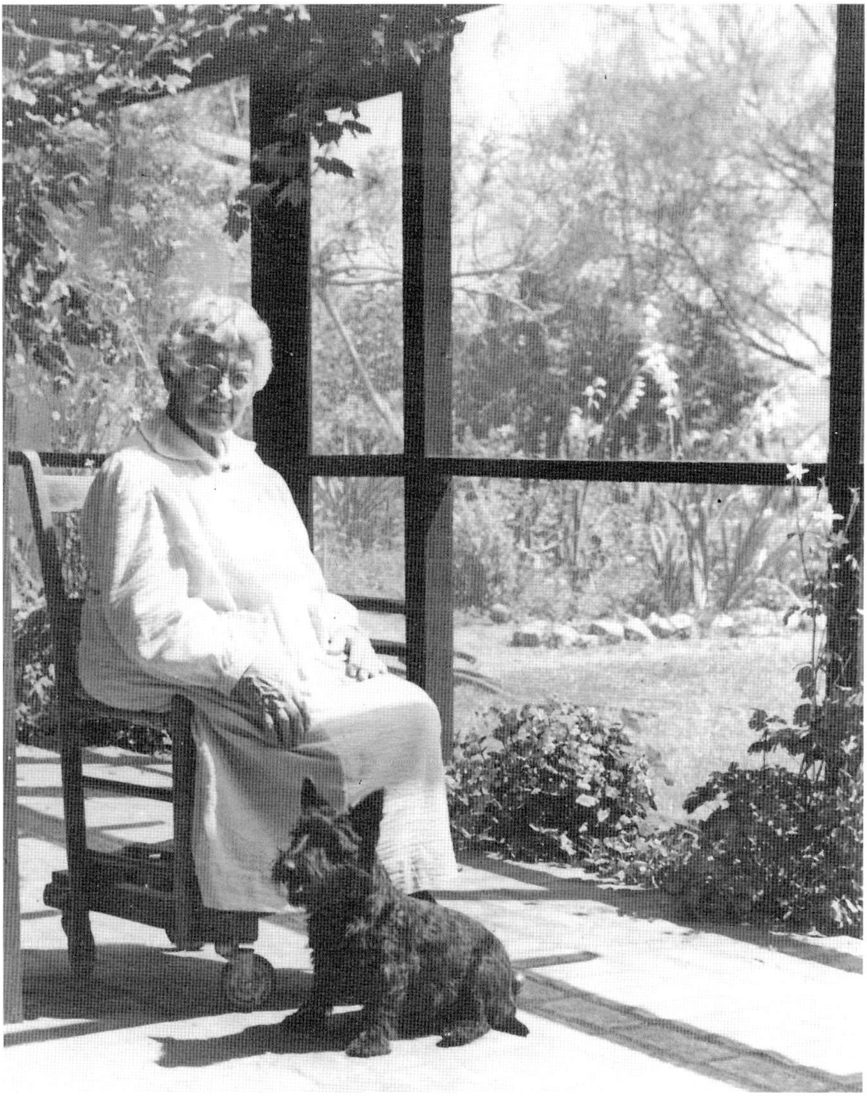

Ella on the screen porch at her son Morris's house in Texas in 1933. This photo was used as her Christmas card that year. *Allen Mitchum Jr.*

In December 1938, Ella's daughter Mary and her siblings threw an eightieth birthday party for Ella that included the family and close friends. Ella's home continued to be a second home for her grandchildren living close by, and she continued to entertain friends for lunch. When World War II arrived, Ella continued to participate with the Woman's Club,

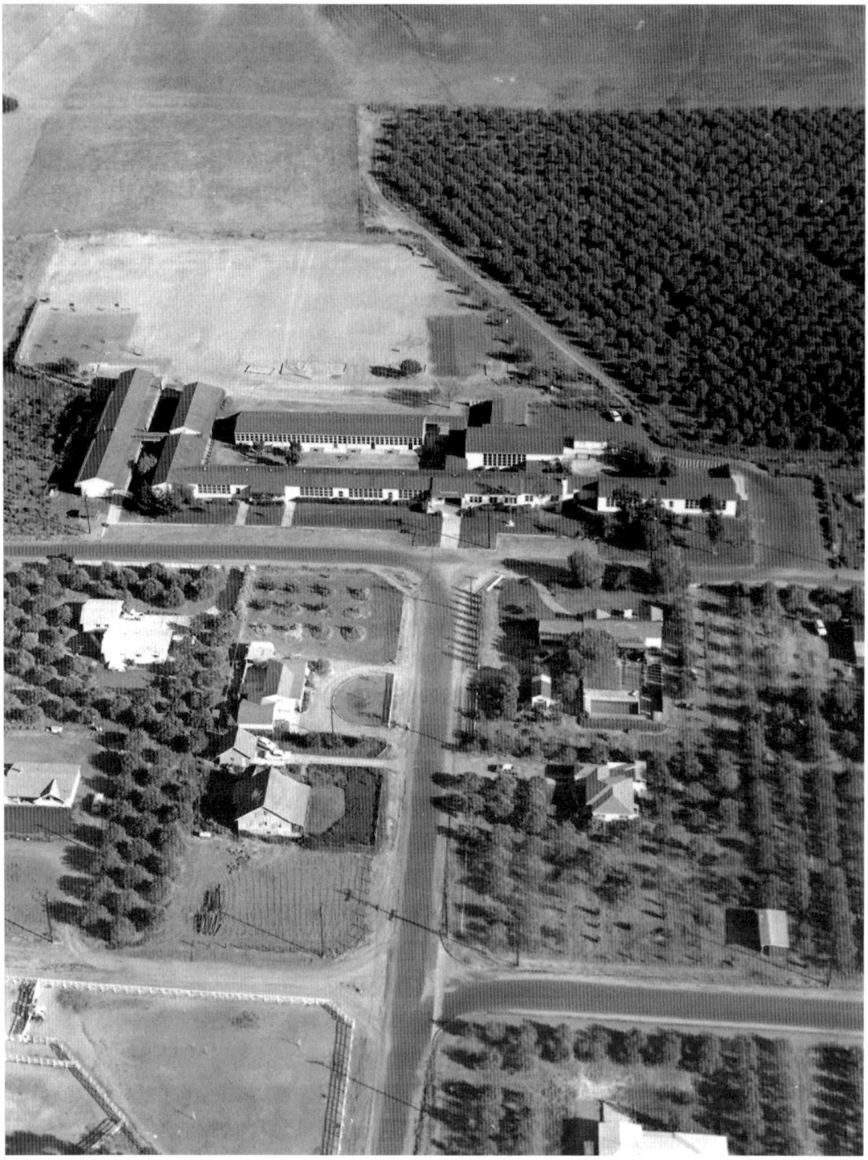

The remnants of the Sweetwater Fruit Company's orchards are still clearly visible in this aerial shot of Ella B. Allen Elementary in the late 1950s. *Bonita Museum & Cultural Center.*

which opened a canteen in its clubhouse. In 1940, she conducted a house-to-house campaign for the Community Chest over the phone. During the war years, Ella's life became very circumspect, as her injured ankle made it increasingly hard for her to get around. Late in 1945, the family decided to sell Los Paderes Ranch, which became part of Singing Hills Country Club, today the Sycuan Golf Resort, where some of the original olive trees still grow.

One of the last public events that Ella attended was in March 1946, when the Sweetwater Woman's Club celebrated its thirty-fifth anniversary. She was one of three original members who were still alive to celebrate, though only she and Mrs. DeWitt Williams were able to attend.

As the population in Chula Vista had grown, so had the number of children at the F Street School, where the Sweetwater Valley kids had been attending since 1922. In December 1945, the school district announced that the new school in Bonita, built on land previously owned by the Sweetwater Fruit Company, would be named in honor of Ella B. Allen. Sadly, we have no account of how Ella received this honor, but she must've been pleased knowing how much education and young people meant to her. On September 15, 1947, the Ella B. Allen Elementary School opened its doors to its first students.

On September 20, 1949, Ella died at her home in Bonita. She left four children, eight grandchildren and four great-grandchildren, as well as countless men, women and children who benefited from her years of tireless service. She was buried at Glen Abbey Cemetery next to her husband, Russell, overlooking their beloved Sweetwater Valley.

Ella was a daughter, wife, mother, sister, teacher, botanist, horticulturalist, gardener, hiker, camper, suffragist, party planner, humanitarian, fundraiser, civic matriarch and a community organizer, but she also was a real person. Mary Ward summed up her estimation of her mother as someone who saw "people as human beings" who "had a real right to the pursuit of happiness." To that end, Ella did what she could to bring that about, whether it involved raising money to help needy mothers and children or throwing a fun party for the community. Her contributions are the kind that are often easy to overlook, but the Sweetwater Valley would've been poorer in many ways had Ella Bradford Copeland Allen not lived there.

6

THE SPRECKELS SCANDALS

Though Bonita is not known for scandal, for a while in the mid-1930s, the scion of a local prominent family brought scandal to this small township. The scandal included trust funds, accusations of infidelity, reconciliations and recriminations, and it opened a window into how some in affluent society lived their lives.

The story starts in 1928 when Albert Wheeler bought 312 acres of Bonita on which he envisioned creating a rich man's mecca that would attract his colleagues and business partners from New York. Wheeler envisioned Bonita Hills containing sizeable homes on spacious lots and he planned on completing a country club and maybe even a racetrack for the members to use. Wheeler employed Albert Treganza as his company architect, and Treganza's first job was building a house for Wheeler on top of the highest hill in the tract, which the developer moved into in 1928. The next home in the development, finished in 1930, was built for Mary Gordon Volkman in a style similar to Wheeler's, on the second-highest hill. Though the Depression was a bit of a setback, Wheeler was content to wait and sell as buyers became available.

By 1932, however, Wheeler had decided to build a house on speculation, hoping to lure potential buyers to his development. It is very possible that Treganza designed the house, but records to prove that point are scarce. The house, on a six-acre plot planted with fruit trees, was finely built with electric heat, telephones, intercoms and attached servants' quarters. Its Italian Mediterranean style included balconies and a loggia, or covered patio, that

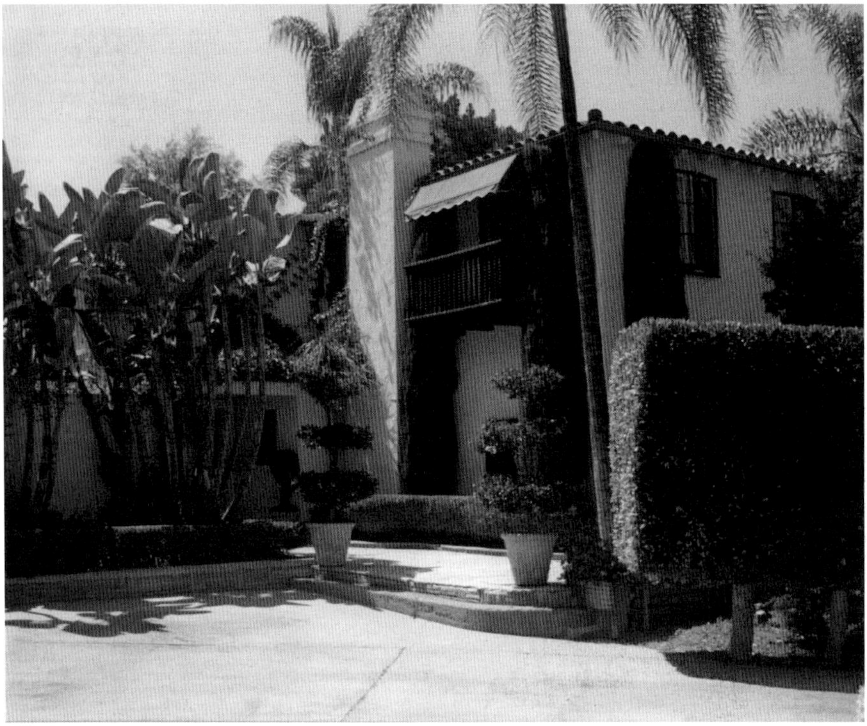

The entryway of the Spreckels House. *Bonita Museum & Cultural Center.*

ran the entire length of the house overlooking a pool. It was richly appointed with massive wooden beams, intricate wrought iron and Italian tile floors.

The house stood empty for several months until purchased in June 1934 by newlyweds Roxana and John D. Spreckels III. John was the great-grandson of Claus Spreckels, who came from meager means but rose to considerable wealth refining sugar. Claus's two sons, John D. and Adolph B., continued in the family business and increased the family's wealth. They had a joint business venture under the name John D. Spreckels and Brothers that did business from San Francisco to San Diego and west to Hawaii, where many of their father's sugar canes were grown.

John Dietrich Spreckels Sr. was well known in San Diego for both his business and civic participation. Though he had visited San Diego as early as 1887, Spreckels moved to San Diego from San Francisco after the 1906 earthquake. He was involved in shipping (he invested in the building of a wharf at the foot of Broadway) and importing as well as publishing. He built the San Diego and Arizona Railway (often called the Impossible Railroad) and acquired the San Diego railway system and converted it to run on electricity. He also built the Spreckels Theatre and the Organ Pavilion in Balboa Park. He acquired control of the Coronado Beach Company, the Hotel del Coronado and Tent City. He became, in short, San Diego's number-one citizen.

John D.'s two eldest sons were John D. Jr. and Adolph B., both children born to money. John D. Jr., more commonly known as "Jack," was quite the socialite and could have had the hand of any of the eligible young women of San Francisco. He won the hand of Edith Marie Huntington, niece of the railroad magnate. Both the Spreckels and Huntington families were members of the San Francisco elite, and together John D. Jr and Edith had three children. Edith divorced John D. Jr. after ten years because of his infidelities with Sadie Wirth. John D. Jr. later married Sadie (who later changed her name to Sidi), and the two had a daughter, Geraldine, in 1919.

John Dolph Spreckels (who is often referred to as John III, though his middle name was not the same as his father's) grew up in wealth. He was born in San Francisco in 1910, but his parents divorced in 1914. He was the youngest child, with an elder brother, Adolph B., and sister, Marie. The divorce agreement was for the children—ten-year-old Marie, eight-year-old Adolph and three-year-old John D. III—to live six months of the year with each parent. Edith married Frank Wakefield on the day her divorce was final in August 1915, and Jack married Sidi Wirth the next month, after getting engaged in February of that year. Both parents fought over custody time, with Edith concerned about Jack turning the kids against her and Jack complaining that she had only kept the children a portion of the time she was supposed to. Jack also claimed that when Edith remarried in 1915, she sent the children to live with his father, John D. Sr. She counter-claimed that Jack had not paid his child support; Jack claimed she should not receive the funds since she was not keeping the children in her care. To describe the interaction as rancorous would not have been out of place.

Family life was thrown into an even bigger jumble when John D. Jr. died in an auto accident. He had just come from visiting one of his oil leases in Taft, California, outside of Bakersfield, when his car skidded off the road and overturned. Locals tried to assist him, but they couldn't revive him. In late 1920, Jack's second wife, Sidi, started the paperwork for a divorce, but her plans were upended by Jack's death. She was his widow, whether she liked it or not.

Two wills were found, but when John D. Jr.'s assets and liabilities were added up, it turned out that he was bankrupt. He had a couple of life insurance policies but nothing else. Into this breach stepped John D. Sr., who was by all accounts a doting grandfather and agreed to include his grandchildren in his will and to offer support to them while he was alive. He also paid settlements to both Edith and Sidi in lieu of any distribution from his son's meager estate. In the months after John D. Jr.'s death, Jack's older children lived with their grandparents in their home on Coronado, something they had done before. John D. III spent some time in military school as well.

After a few years of calm, John D. Sr.'s wife, Lillie, died in January 1924, and John D. Sr. died in June 1926 after a lengthy illness. John D. Sr.'s will divided his estate equally among his children and grandchildren. The grandchildren's portions were to be kept in a trust until the youngest, Geraldine, reached eighteen. John D. III did not enter college when he graduated from high school as one might expect, and in 1930, he was living as a boarder in San Francisco, listing no employment. He had a couple of minor run-ins with the law, speeding tickets and the like. To add yet another

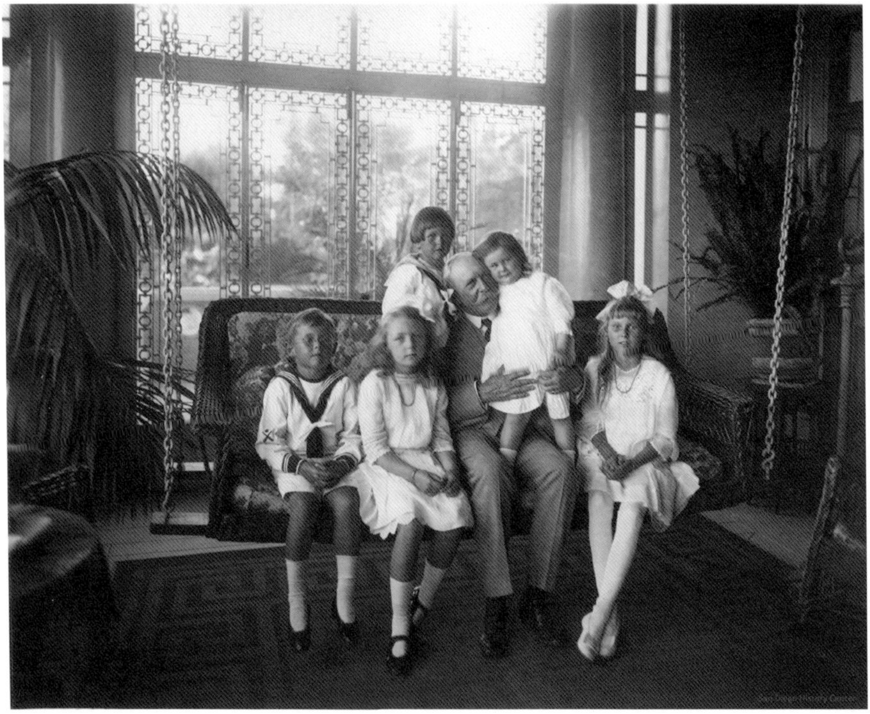

John D. Spreckels Sr. and his grandchildren at his home on Coronado in 1914. John D. III is the boy standing next to John D. Sr. *San Diego History Center*.

misery to his life, John D. III's mother, Edith, died in an auto accident in February 1931, leaving John D. III without any parental supervision.

Roxana Gloria Brown's upbringing was far different. Her father, a Baptist minister, began preaching in Marshall, Michigan, in 1911. She was the second child, with an elder sister, Sara, and a younger brother, Giles. The family remained in Michigan until 1918, when they moved to Covina, where Roxana's father, A. Watson Brown, took over the First Baptist Church. In 1920, they moved to Sacramento, where Reverend Watson took over the Calvary Baptist Church. In 1928, Roxana graduated from Sacramento High School, where she had been involved in debate, student council and tennis. The Browns moved to National City in June 1930, when Reverend Brown took over the First Baptist Church. Roxana was enrolled in San Diego State College.

In early 1932, John D. III was set up on a blind date with an eligible young lady of National City. Roxana was twenty-one years old and considered quite a beautiful and accomplished young woman. It was, as they say, love at first sight, and the couple eloped to Yuma, Arizona, where they were married on February 8, 1932, two days after John D. III's twenty-first birthday. Though the wedding looked like an elopement, Roxana's father told the newspaper that it was done with his full consent. Roxana later stated that she had her first hard alcohol on that date, not surprising for the daughter of a Baptist minister. It also cannot be ignored that marrying an heir of the Spreckels family was quite a triumph.

After their sudden wedding, the couple lived first with the Spreckels family on Coronado. They left to sail in their yacht, the *Cal Chief*, in August 1932 with their mascot, Swastika, an English black and tan. They lived on the yacht until the end of 1932, but later moved back onto Coronado. In June 1934, Mr. and Mrs. John D. Spreckels III purchased the house in Bonita Hills from Albert Wheeler. The arrival of members of such an illustrious family must have delighted the local residents.

Horse racing was a passion of the Spreckels men, including John D. Jr.'s brother, Adolph, who had been an investor in the Agua Caliente racetrack in Tijuana. John D. Sr. and Adolph provided an infusion of cash after flooding in 1916 devastated the original track at Agua Caliente. John D. III was no exception, and he quickly set about building a barn with four box stalls and two paddocks to accommodate his racehorses, which had recently been kept on leased land on the Silver Strand south of Coronado. In addition to the horses he had in San Diego, John D. III had stables in Arlington, Texas, where he also maintained a home, for a total of sixteen horses.

John D. III hired the best trainers for his horses, including Tom Smith, who would go on to great success as the trainer of Seabiscuit. John D. III had also heard that monkeys made good companion animals for horses so he purchased a brown-faced organ grinder (Capuchin) monkey to join his stables. He traveled to San Francisco to pick up the animal, but even with lots of coaxing, the monkey never got along with the horses. It was removed from the stables to a cage on the patio of the Bonita house, but it was able to open its cage and escape to pull all the tail feathers out of Mrs. Spreckels's prized macaw. The Spreckelses gave the monkey to Roxana's brother, Giles, who kept it for the next forty years.

John D. III had luck with Bissagos and Quickaway, winning races at Agua Caliente and Tanforan. Quickaway collapsed after a race and was put down, but John D. III continued to buy, race and win with his horses. Disagreements with the stewards running the Agua Caliente track may have been the reason that John D. III decided to move the rest of his horses to Arlington, Texas, which he started early in 1934. But racing horses has always been an expensive sport, and it remained the case for John D. III.

Success on the track, however, contradicted the state of the newlyweds' home. Just four months after moving into the Bonita Hills house, in October 1934, Roxana sued for divorce, citing cruelty and seeking $1,000 a month for support. Included in the cruelty charges were accusations that John D. III spent too much time away from home with his horses. John D. III countered that Roxana's movie contract was interfering with their marriage. (She had made her first screen test in March 1934.) John denied the charges, but a judge ordered him to pay $460 a month support pending the divorce, and the transfer of his portion of his inheritance was put on hold pending the trial.

As it turns out, Roxana was pregnant, and on March 24, 1935, Elsie LaMarr Spreckels was born. The divorce suit was dropped in favor of reconciliation, but by August, the divorce proceedings had been reinstated. Roxana had given John D. III an ultimatum—either give up his horses or his family. John D. III, who had been living on and off in Arlington, Texas, took this opportunity to move to Reno, Nevada. Up until this time, Roxana and Elsie had been living in the house in Bonita Hills, but as the judge made clear in his ruling later in 1935, the house had mostly been abandoned.

In a move to circumvent Roxana's California divorce proceedings, John D. III used his residence in Reno to start a default (no fault) divorce proceeding there, but that suit was later disallowed. It's clear from the court transcripts that he was trying to give up as little of his inheritance as possible. After yet another property settlement failed in February 1936, a divorce suit was begun in Los Angeles. Roxana continued to allege that in addition to abandoning her and Elsie for the company of his horses, John D. III threatened her with guns while intoxicated and subjected her to verbal abuse, including saying that he wished the child had died. She also claimed he was frequently in the company of other women and gambled large sums of money. Under questioning, John D. III did admit that the couple had jointly run through the $225,000 that he had received when he turned twenty-one in 1931, because "our mode of living required it." He also admitted that he wasn't "equipped to hold a regular job." In the divorce settlement, Roxana got custody of Elsie, with payments of $500 per month for her and $100 for the child. John D. III was obliged to pay Roxana's lawyers' fees of $15,000. Their divorce was finalized in 1936, but there were continued squabbles over the property settlement for several years. In 1937, the trust that John D. Sr. had set up was terminated, and each of Jack's children received around $1 million, which must have cheered John D. III up a bit.

In March 1937, however, an auction was held on the lawn at the Bonita Hills property to sell the house and its contents, which had been attached for unpaid legal fees left over from the 1936 divorce case. The auction was advertised in the newspaper as the "John D. Spreckels III Country Estate." The house, described as a "palatial Mediterranean type San Diego County home," had previously been valued at $20,000 and was for sale, but no bids were accepted that day. The house's contents were also for sale, set out around the estate like a high-end garage sale. Furnishings that sold included a French bed set, a living room and dining room set, rugs, a radio and a Westinghouse refrigerator and electric stove. The house was sold through a private sale in the following weeks.

In 1938, Roxana waived her right to regular alimony in exchange for a settlement of $33,900, most of that going into a trust from which she could live, and her monthly child support was increased to $225. John D. III received residual amounts of the trust, $12,000 in cash and 529 shares of Spreckels company stock.

Both Roxana and John D. III were to have continued marital troubles. Roxana continued to pursue a movie career after her divorce, followed by a short-lived marriage to businessman Ogden K. Hunsaker of Pasadena in 1939, and then she married Ray Harold Babcock in 1942. In 1949, she married for the final time, this time to Walter Hirtenstein. They lived in San Diego, and she died in 1970, he in 1972. Roxana's parents and siblings all lived much more conventional lives, mostly staying in National City.

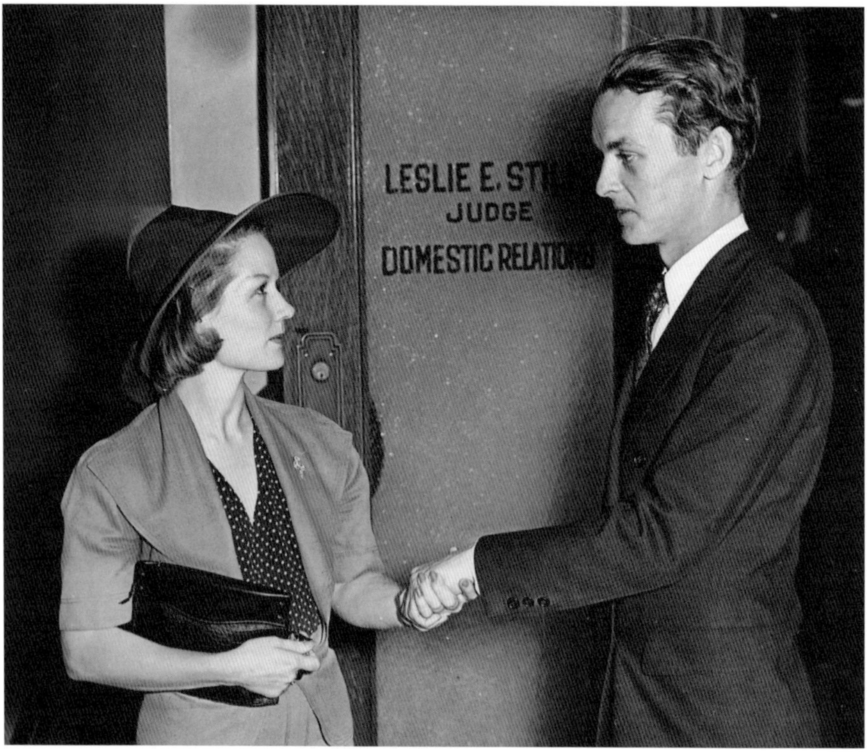

Roxana G. Brown and John D. Spreckels III shake hands on the day of their final divorce settlement in 1938. *Author's collection.*

John D. III's troubles lasted longer and were more widely covered in the news. In July 1937, he married Mary Lavinia Miller, a dancer. In 1944, John D. III enlisted in the navy, and he was eventually sent to the U.S. Navy Training School in Newport, Rhode Island. While he was in training school, Mary sued for divorce in August 1944. As would continue with his subsequent divorces, Mary charged that John D. III drank to excess and was violent, as well as profligate with money, and that she found him with another woman when she came to meet him on furlough. John D. III was assigned in October 1944 to the newly commissioned USS *Panamint*, an amphibious force command ship, as a bugler, second class. He spent a year on board in the Pacific, served during the Battle of Okinawa and was on board when the formal surrender of Northern Japan occurred on the decks of the *Panamint* in September 1945. He remained on the *Panamint* until late in November 1945, when he was sent to Camp Shoemaker in California and subsequently discharged from the navy. In March 1945, the divorce was finalized, and Mary received a $100,000 property settlement. She also explored an acting career.

In April 1946, John D. III married Lou Dell Breese, who had already had six husbands, a fact he didn't find out about until they ended up in divorce court two years later. On September 11, Lou was seriously injured in an automobile accident in Barstow, California. She was on her way to Las Vegas to visit John D. III when the car overturned. She recovered, but by May 1947, Lou was alleging that John D. III had left her. Within a week, they reconciled. In August, they had their first public fight, in the middle of Santa Monica Boulevard, which caused motorists to either stop or drive around the fighting couple. In September, their second fracas, which forced Lou to seek a divorce, involved John D. III hitting her with a fire poker in their home in Arcadia. He was later acquitted of assault with a deadly weapon but was forced to pay a fine for disturbing the peace. They divorced in 1948, with her receiving a $50,000 settlement. John D. III continued to pursue success at horse racing, but he was not increasing his fortune. This was clearly the most volatile of John D. III's marriages.

In October 1949, John D. III married Margaret Lee Peters. They had a son, John Dolph Spreckels IV, born in January 1951 but were in divorce court just two months after his birth. Margaret filed for divorce, saying she feared for her safety and that of the child because he hit her and drank excessively. He was, at the time, working as a night clerk at a hotel. At the time of divorce from Margaret, he was still paying Roxana $225 a month in child support, Mary Lavinia $206 a month as part of her $100,000 settlement and settled with Lou Dell for a lump sum of $52,900, as well as paying $100 to Margaret for support of his son.

In December 1955, John D. Spreckels III appeared in court in Seattle to petition to change his name to John D. Smith. He was working as a cabinet salesman for his brother, Adolph, who operated a custom cabinet shop in Seattle. He complained, "Prospective employers and fellow workers look upon me as a financier and playboy," which was not true. He was paying twenty-five dollars a month to the government for back taxes. He was tired of the fame that his famous name placed on him. The judge agreed to his wishes. He left the courthouse just plain John D. Smith.

John D. Smith lived out the next twenty years quietly in Washington, eventually moving to Kititas, a small plains community in central Washington. John died in June 1973, though his grave marker lists his name as John Dolph Spreckels III and honors his military service. The children had uneventful lives, especially compared with their parents. Elsie LaMarr

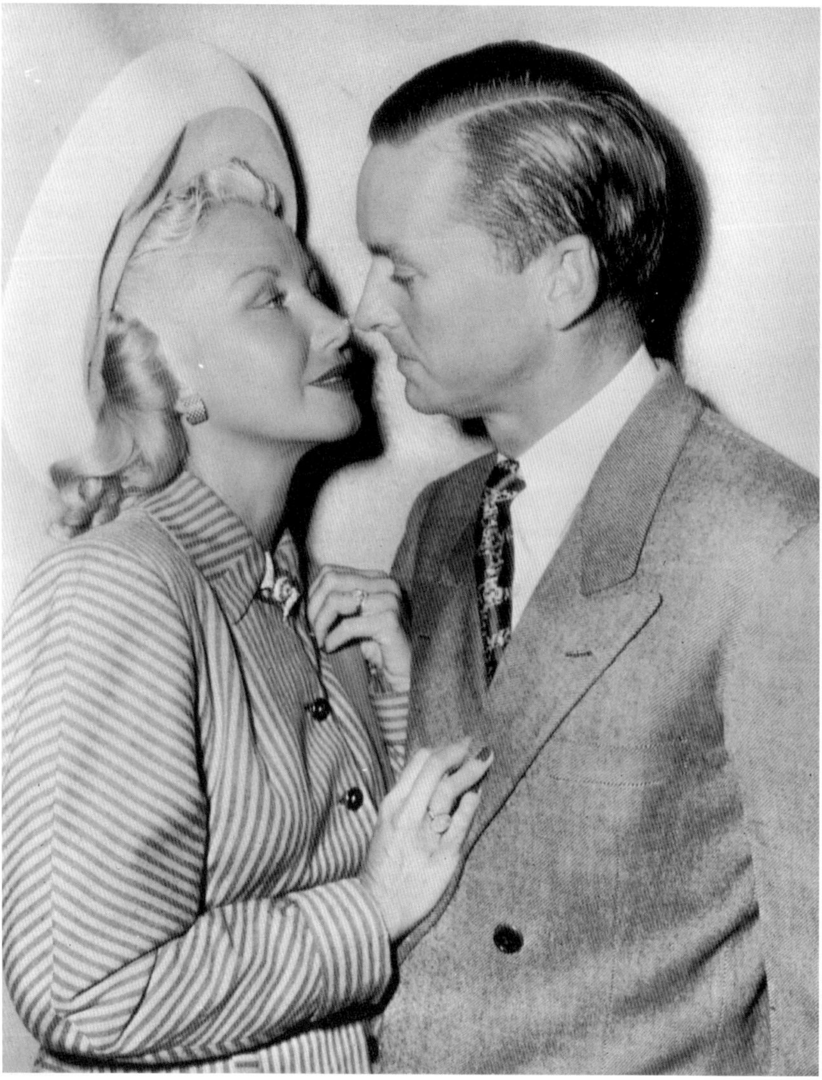

Lou Dell Breese and John D. Spreckels III after pleading guilty to charges of intoxication after their arrests from fighting in the street in August 1947. *Author's collection.*

Spreckels married a man she met at the University of Colorado. John Dolph Spreckels IV lived most of his life in California and died in La Mesa in 2006.

Though Roxana and John D. Spreckels III lived in the Bonita Hills house for less than a year, the Spreckels name has been associated with it ever since. Certainly, the prominence of the Spreckels family as well as the public marital troubles that Roxana and John D. III had while living in Bonita made it plausible that the Spreckels name would continue to be associated with the house. (Later residents included Billy Casper, the golfer, who was deeply involved in designing the Bonita Country Club, now the Chula Vista Golf Course.) But either way, the beautiful house on the hill conveys a bit of the Spreckels legacy to Bonita.

7

THE VALLEY'S HAPPENING PLACE

Whatever Happened to the Sunnyside Steak Ranch?

In the years before World War II, Bonita and Sunnyside were very quiet places. There were two country stores, the Bonita and Sunnyside Schoolhouses and the Sweetwater Fruit Company's group of buildings. There were homes and orchards but not much else.

In 1876, J.C. Frisbie bought a 246-acre piece of land in the Sweetwater Valley, where he sowed a multitude of plants and trees on a farmstead he called Sunnyside. Frisbie was very successful with his crops, being especially known for his raisins and oranges. He moved to San Diego in 1881 but retained the land, continuing to grow crops. He created a map of the Villa of Sunnyside, as he called it, during the land boom of the 1880s, with seven parcels totaling over 85 acres. Frisbie sold a 20-acre parcel at the corner of Bonita and Central to Stephen W. Morgan in 1890, roughly the property bordered by Bonita Road, Frisbie Street and Central Avenue. In 1892, Sunnyside had a combination post office and country store, and it remained even less settled than Bonita for many years.

In 1932, a group of folks, many of whom were members of the Sunnyside Friends Church, started the Sunnyside Friendship Club for social entertainment and recreation. For their first outing, the group of forty took a moonlight cruise on San Diego Bay, after which they returned to Al Swanson's place in Sunnyside for coffee, sandwiches and dancing.

Algot Swanson had come to the United States from Sweden in 1888. His family included his three brothers—David, Carl and Victor—and his sister, Nannie. Al lived in Minnesota for over twenty years before he arrived in San Diego in 1912. He worked as a butcher and, by 1918, had become the manager of the La Mesa Meat Market and was married to Caroline. Tragedy struck the couple when Caroline died suddenly in 1919. Al continued to live in La Mesa and served on the city's board of trustees. (His home from that time, at 4580 Palm Avenue, is on the list of La Mesa's Designated Historical Landmarks.)

In 1911, Al's sister, Nannie, married Edward Anderson, and in 1920, they left Minnesota with their daughter and came to California. Edward was one of twelve children, including five brothers, many of whom ended up living in the Bonita-Sunnyside area. In the early 1920s, Edward and Al went into business together in a secondhand furniture store in downtown. The business, which eventually became Anderson Brothers Furniture, continued in the family until the mid-1960s, as a regular source of income and employment for the large family

In 1924, Al, Nannie and Edward bought the twenty-acre plot of land from Stephen Morgan's heirs. They divided the property so that Al's plot included an existing small house on Frisbie Street, one that had been moved to the property in the 1890s. At this time, Al listed his occupation as rancher.

Al, one of the original members of the Friendship Club, had 3.4 acres of land just west of the Sunnyside Friends Church, which was then located at Dory Street and Bonita Road. (The church building was moved across the valley in 1980.) In the next few years, he hosted a number of events for the Friendship Club and the church, as well as the local Pinochle Club, usually involving food and dancing. The original outdoor venue included picnic tables, a fire pit and a dance pavilion, all built by Al.

In 1929, Edward Anderson bought an even larger piece of pastureland on the north side of the Sweetwater River, creating a subdivision he called Sweetwater Manor. He bought a few small houses from a failed subdivision and moved them to his land. Al worked on this project with Edward.

The popularity of Al's party space prompted him to enlarge the dancing floor in 1935 and create an enclosed space referred to as the Clubhouse. By 1936, locals had begun to refer to Al's property as the Sunnyside Friendship Clubhouse or the Swan Inn. It had not quite yet become a restaurant, but it was still a busy place, hosting Friendship Club events as well as birthday parties, family reunions and wedding receptions. Clubs from outside Bonita and Sunnyside started to rent the space at the Swan Inn in the late 1930s, and local bands like Frank English and his Blue Notes, Harlan Skinner and His Band and the San Miguel Hill Billies played for dances.

In 1936, Algot and Edward Anderson created the Sunny Vista subdivision. This sixty-four-acre tract ran along the crest of the hill where Pepper Tree Lane and Vista Drive intersect. Edward Anderson finished his home there in 1937 and used it as a sort of model home for other prospective buyers. Al never built a home at Sunny Vista, but he did work with Edward on the other homes there. The late 1930s wasn't a great time to be selling land, but a handful of homes were built, all with commanding views of the Sweetwater Valley. An extension of the road from G Street, Pepper Tree Lane, was built to give access to the area from Chula Vista. Howard and Agnes Berkey, who had formerly run the Bonita Store, were early builders in the subdivision.

In 1938, the Sweetwater Men's Club organized and started holding monthly meetings at the Swan Inn. (Al Swanson was also a charter member of the Men's Club.) In addition, the Swan Inn hosted events by the Chula Vista Sport Fishing Club, the San Diego Flying Club, the South Bay Piston and Revolver Club and the United Parcel Service's company picnic. In the years before World War II, the Swan Inn transitioned from a local occasional hangout to a genuine establishment. If it happened in the valley, it happened at the Swan Inn. In the 1940 census, Al updated his occupation to owner of a "public dance pavilion."

In the late spring of 1942, Al Swanson was sick for some weeks, spending two months in the Paradise Valley sanitarium and several more weeks living at Nannie's house before returning to his own home. He was not a young man at sixty-two, and he realized it was time to retire and find a successor to take over the club, which had become an integral part of the community. In 1944, Alec and Ruth Burnett took over managing the Inn, which continued to host events and serve customers, giving Al the chance to travel. Sadly, Al's retirement was cut short when during one of his vacations, he died in a car accident in Washington in July 1947. He was buried at Glen Abby Cemetery, overlooking the valley where he had spent a large part of his life.

In 1945, Al and the Andersons had sold the portion of his property that contained the restaurant. After Al's death, those owners sold to Harry Irwin. Irwin, who was an out-of-town owner, put Mr. and Mrs. C.M. Nelson in charge of management of the eatery. Under the Nelsons' management, the place went through a series of name changes as they tried to get their bearings, including the Sunnyside Club and the Sunnyside Tavern. Advertising appears for the eatery, something that had not previously been done, and it often included the Swan Inn name as well. The ads highlighted music and dancing and an "experienced chef" in the kitchen. The newly remodeled interior of the restaurant included the addition of a cocktail lounge, giving Bonita its first, and for many years only, bar.

In 1949, Wayne "Buzz" Wendling and his wife, Francis, bought the restaurant business. They decided that the place needed a complete makeover, so they again redecorated, and as part of highlighting Kansas City steaks and chops on the menu, they renamed the restaurant the Sunnyside Steak Ranch. Their advertising slogan was "When in the Mood for Grog & Food." Buzz had been in the restaurant business for many years, primarily in Los Angeles. They converted the dance floor to table space, increasing their capacity.

In 1951 and 1952, the Steak Ranch hosted the firemen's balls, raising money for Bonita's volunteer fire department. Though there was a change of ownership in 1953, the only major change the new owners made was to bring charcoal grilling back to the club, something that Al had previously done outdoors. With the surge in the local population and the increase in families dining out, this is the era in which the popularity and renown of the Sunnyside Steak Ranch took off. It's also the era when the place got its reputation as a roadhouse, though of quite a tame variety. We know that Al Swanson hosted the Sweetwater Pinochle Club for many events, as early as 1932, and that he allowed the poker games held by the Sweetwater Men's Club after meetings. What the stakes were for these games is anybody's guess, but during the Depression, it couldn't have been much. Whether there was alcohol in the early years is unknown, thought we do know Al hosted many events for the Friends Church, which would have been unlikely to serve alcohol.

In 1960, Doc and Janie Maurer bought the Sunnyside Steak Ranch, both the business and the property. The Maurers did a fair amount of remodeling and redecorating, including introducing the brass lamps that became the Steak Ranch's logo, and replacing the dance floor that had been covered by tables for a decade. Doc said that wanted his customers to "feel like they had just joined some good friends for dinner," so he worked hard to keep the atmosphere friendly and downhome. In 1961, the Steak Ranch first advertised using a street address—5170 Bonita Road—something it had never done before. Previously, patrons were told to head four miles east of Chula Vista on Bonita Road and look for the place next to the Sunnyside Post Office.

Doc had been raised on a sheep and cattle ranch in Wyoming and had been around animals his whole life. He got a degree in veterinary medicine from Washington State College in 1938 and then traveled the "bush

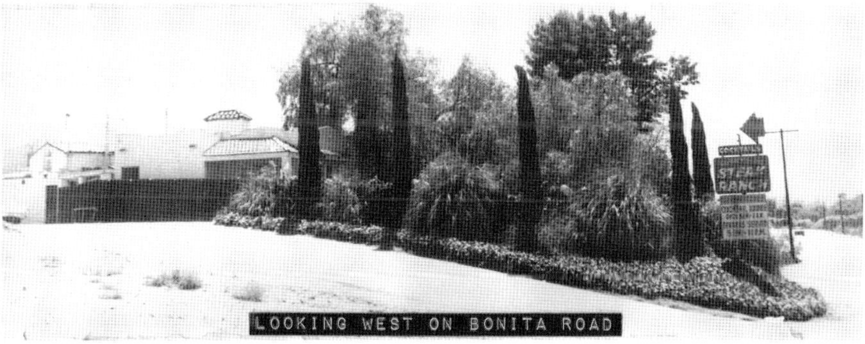

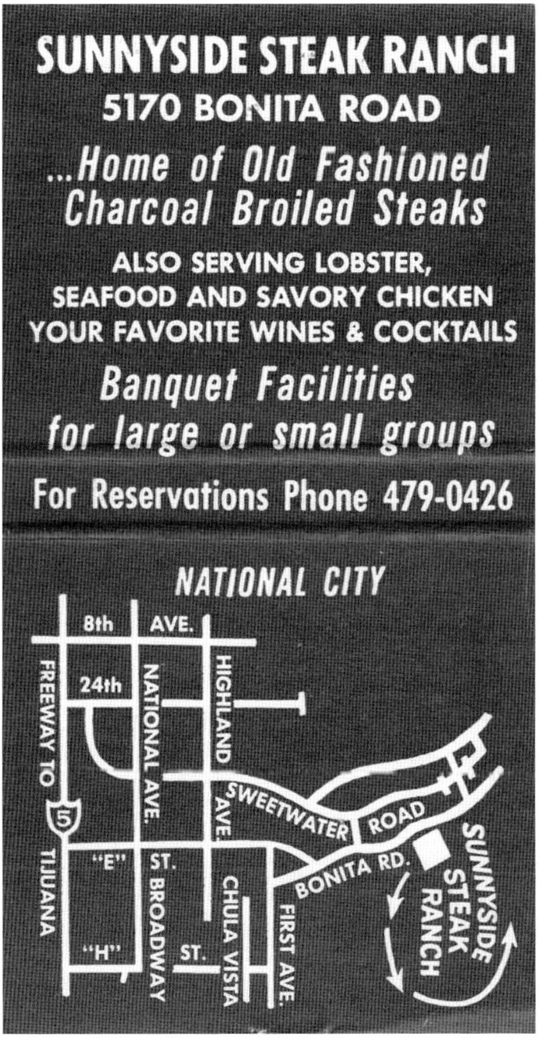

Above: The Sunnyside Steak Ranch in the 1960s. *Morrison Family Collection*.

Left: Inside of a matchbook from the Sunnyside Steak Ranch showing the map. *Author's collection*.

league" racetracks of Montana, hoping to one day be part of the racing establishment. After five years of army service in World War II, he settled in Chula Vista in 1946. Doc co-founded the first veterinary clinic in Chula Vista in 1947 with Dr. Nathan Burg on National Avenue after resigning from his position as meat inspector with the health department. (Doc and Nathan had gone to Washington State together.) One day, Doc got an emergency call from Caliente Racetrack. The regular vet had broken his leg, and management needed someone to step in temporarily. He did so and remained the track vet into the 1970s. He oversaw a staff of three, taking and testing samples for the horses preparing to race. So he found his way into racing accidentally. After a Sunday at the track, Doc and Janie frequented local dining establishments like the Silver Dollar and the Sunnyside Steak Ranch. When the opportunity came up to buy the Steak Ranch, Doc, who had previous history as a business owner with his veterinary clinics, decided to take the plunge into the restaurant business.

Initially, the entire Maurer clan worked at the Steak Ranch, with Janie acting as the manager and hostess and their daughter Jo lending a hand when she wasn't taking classes at San Diego State. Glenn Morrison, who had been the host at the Steak House, joined the clan in 1963 when he married Jo. In keeping with the friendly atmosphere, the Steak House invited the locals to spend holidays there, offering special menus for Valentine's Day, Mother's Day, Father's Day, Thanksgiving and New Year's Eve. The Maurers brought in an organist for weeknight entertainment and hosted a band on weekends for dancing. The facility could seat 250 people, with a banquet space for 125. The Maurers also introduced some signature foods in addition to the regular steak and chops, including frog legs, pots of peppered vegetables on the table and their signature house dressing, a blue cheese vinaigrette. The house salad dressing and the pepper pots on every table became known far and wide, though the recipes were closely guarded secrets.

By the late 1960s, the Maurers had become involved in other development plans, including one to build a restaurant. The Valley Shadows on San Ysidro Boulevard was part of a complex that also included the new Valli-Hi Motel. One restaurant in the family seemed enough for Doc, and in 1971, the Maurers sold the Sunnyside Steak Ranch business to Ken and Sally Lester. The Lesters continued on for a while, but they ended up in divorce court in 1972. The restaurant business being what it is, bankruptcy caught up with the Maurers, and by 1973, the Sunnyside Steak Ranch had closed. Doc and Janie continued to live in the Bonita area for many years, Doc continuing to assist his friends and neighbors with their pets.

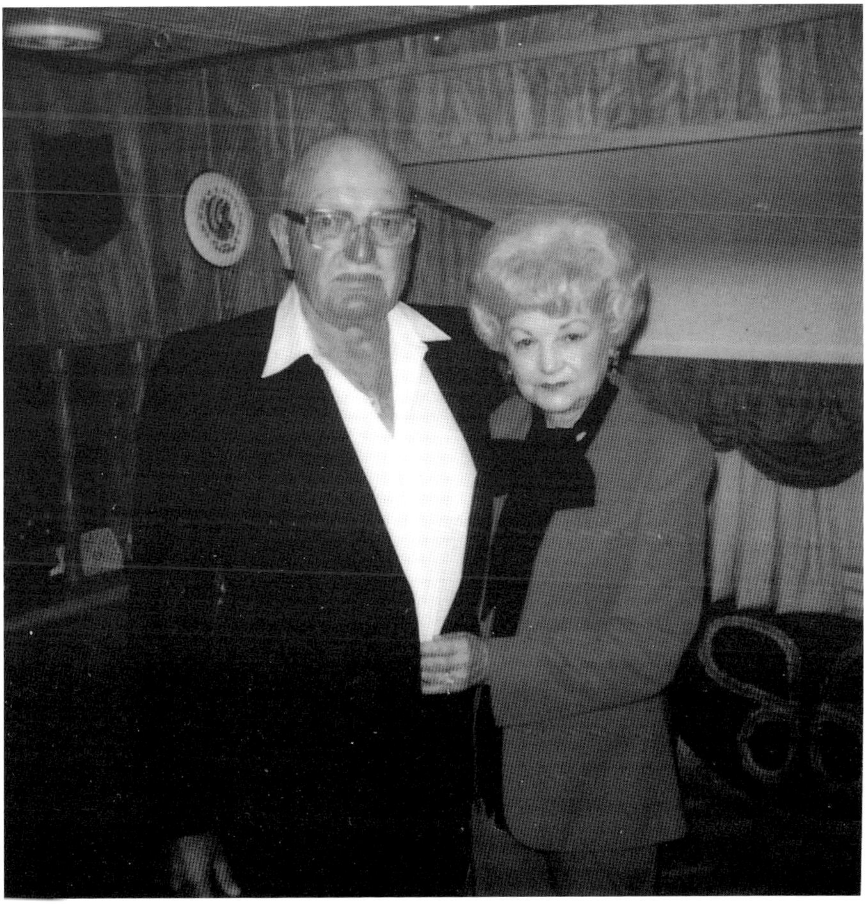

Doc and Janie Maurer in the 1980s. *Morrison Family Collection.*

The property was sold to Mascot Realty in September 1974, which was fortunate, as the empty building had been vandalized and set on fire over the months the restaurant had been closed. Though several local groups wanted to buy and reuse the old building, none had the $30,000 that refurbishing would have cost. As the building was being dismantled in July 1975, John Tingley, who for many years owned a produce stand in the valley and was better known as Farmer John, was interested in buying the vacant land for his stand. Instead, it was purchased by Richard and Eva Harvey. The Harveys had opened Bonita Home, Garden and Pool Supplies in 1974, located in the shopping center at Bonita Road and Central Avenue.

In August 1976, the Harveys celebrated the grand opening of their new location, built on the site of the Swan Inn but situated slightly differently on the lot. In early 1978, the property was again divided into a west and east parcel, each of about one acre. The Harveys' store was located on the easterly parcel, with the west parcel being sold off for development. The Harveys decided to close their business in late 1978.

In December 1980, the Sunnyside Steak Ranch rose again, the brainchild of Bob and Patti Basile. Bob and his dad, Don, had come to San Diego to take over running the South Bay Speedway. Though Bob had never been in the previous incarnation of the Sunnyside Steak Ranch, what he had heard made him believe it should be resurrected. Bob's in-laws, the Greasers, were from Sunnyside and lived just around the corner from the original Steak Ranch. They and many other locals still missed their hangout, and hopes were high for a successful relaunch. Bob knew that his job promoting the Speedway was going to end, as he knew the Speedway had lost its lease, and he thought reopening the Steak House would be a great challenge. (The Speedway finally closed in 1983.) Though the nursery building would need work to be a restaurant, what it did have going for it was the original location. During the five months of renovations, Bob added a kitchen on the east side of the building and, to the south side, a space for a bar. The custom-made eighteen-foot-long bar would allow for many patrons enjoying drinks.

Bob Basile's plan had everything going for it, but fate dealt him a blow. After applying for his liquor license in July 1980, he should've had it long before Christmas, but that was not the case. It was halfway into 1981 when the license arrived. And it's true that the lack of a liquor license can ruin a restaurant's bottom line. Between the lack of a liquor license and a downturn in the economy, Basile ended up running behind on his rent. The landlord, without much pity, evicted Basile after only one missed payment. The reborn Sunnyside Steak Ranch was no more. Bob returned to race promoting, and his company, Sunnyside Promotions, continues to this day. He had the bar disassembled and moved into his house, where it exists in three sections (a bar, an end table and an office desk). But he still wonders what could've been with the reborn Sunnyside Steak Ranch.

In March 1982, Murrieta's Mexican Food & Steak Restaurant opened in Basile's former restaurant. Olivia Ferreras worked in the restaurant industry for twenty years before she opened Murrieta's. She named her restaurant for Joaquin Murrieta, the Mexican hero, because she was tired of "Casa this, and Casa that" she said. Her recipes concentrated on the regions of

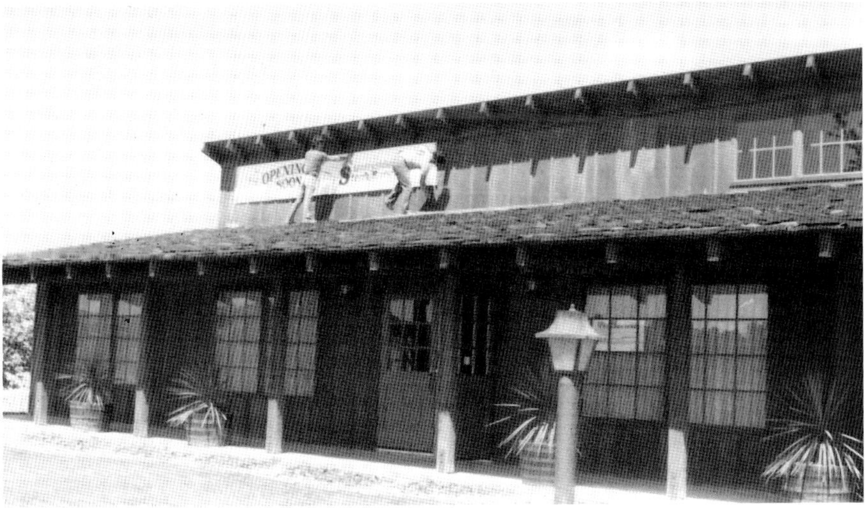

The Sunnyside Steak Ranch, as reborn in 1980, had a more rustic design than the original. *Bob and Patty Basile.*

Jalisco and Sonora, and she was involved in all the decisions about her café. Whatever choices she made, she must have done something right, because in 2018, Murrieta's celebrated its thirty-sixth anniversary.

So, yes, there was quite a renowned place in Sunnyside, first known as the Swan Inn and later the Sunnyside Steak Ranch. In later years, the little burg of Sunnyside was subsumed into Bonita, an effect that was amplified by Sunnyside losing its own postmark in 1974 when the post office was combined with Bonita's. The Sunnyside Store was torn down in 2011 and replaced by a 7-11, leaving no trace of the little community that had been. But for many years, the real happening spot in the Sweetwater Valley wasn't in Bonita, it was in Sunnyside.

8

THE SWEETWATER MEN'S CLUB

We Had One of Those?

Of many organizations that have existed in the valley over the years, the Sweetwater Women's Club and the Sweetwater Valley Civic Association are well known. There have been church groups and service clubs and social clubs like the Sunnyside Pinochle Club and the Merry-Go-Round Club, but not well known is the Sweetwater Valley Men's Club. Now it would not be far wrong to call the Sweetwater Men's Club, as it was more commonly called, a social club. But that would also negate the good that the club did in the valley and the camaraderie it afforded its members.

In the 1930s, there were around four hundred people living in the valley. We don't really know exactly how the Men's Club started, but we know that Al Swanson had to be involved. His was then was the only non-church establishment in the valley that could host such a group. From its inception, the Men's Club held its regular meetings and special events at the Swan Inn. Al Swanson was one of the original members, and it would've been easy for him to provide a space for the group to meet. In 1938, he did just that for the first gathering of twenty-nine members, with Ray MacDonald elected as president. In December of that year, the Men's Club held the first of its annual Christmas parties. The Christmas party was the one event where the members' wives were invited.

Over the years, the Men's Club roster contained the names of most of the well-known residents of the valley. Morris and Richard Allen were both members, as were Averell and Emil Anderson, Charles and Fred Higgins,

Scofield Bonnet, John Esterbloom, Edgar Boal, Steve Gassaway and Lara Good. Membership numbers were as high as eighty-five, though fifty to fifty-five was the average, with average meeting attendance at thirty-five to forty. Keeping the membership up was a repeated concern in the minutes throughout the years after World War II.

During the war, the club became more civic minded in its operations. It manned a listening post tuned to the sheriff's department radio bands. Since the Sweetwater Valley did not create wards as part of the civil defense operations like Chula Vista did, the Men's Club monitoring the radio acted as such and would've alerted residents in the event of an attack. The Men's Club also was involved in other civil defense programs like drives to collect scrap metal and kitchen grease.

During the war years, Al Swanson retired from running the Swan's Inn. At that time, the Men's Club moved its meetings to the Sweetwater Woman's Club clubhouse, where members paid a monthly rent for use of the space and kitchen, allowing them to cook their own meals. They created teams to take over preparing food and traded off the responsibilities for the dinners. The group continued to have interesting speakers about the Atlas Missile and about local election issues like waterfront bonds. Colonel Brian Kearney, commandant of the Chula Vista National Guard, came to speak on universal military training. In 1949, when members found out that the construction of Allen School did not outfit the field for softball, the club planned a Diamond Ball to raise funds to assist in equipping the field. The Men's Club even sponsored a boys' softball team.

We know a bit more about the club in the years after the war because the minutes were donated to the Bonita Museum & Cultural Center. The minutes are reasonably interesting to read, as the secretaries inject their own personalities into their recording of matters before the club. Members of the club continued to raise issues about the safety of the valley roads, especially the intersection at Otay and Bonita Roads and of the necessity of better street lines and directional signs. The group voted to change the selection of dinner responsibilities to picking from a hat, with names only returning to the hat once everyone had prepared a meal for the group.

At the meeting in January 1950, Scofield Bonnet, a member for many years, brought up the possibility of forming a volunteer fire department. Scofield, whose family owned the house that had been built by Robert Winsor in 1913, had a small Christmas tree fire the month previous. Scofield had been able to put the fire out, but he was concerned that the only fire protection for Bonita would have had to come from the California Division of Forestry's station on East J Street in Chula Vista. The club members agreed that it was a good idea to look into and formed an action committee to research forming a volunteer fire department. By the next meeting, the groundwork for the volunteer fire department had been laid, with the incorporation papers signed on February 14, 1950. Four of the five organizers and six of the original sixteen volunteer firefighters were members of the Men's Club. Startup costs for the Upper Sweetwater Valley Volunteer Fire Department were determined to be around $700. A member of the forestry department spoke about fire protection at the February meeting as well.

The Sweetwater Fruit Company had previously donated a five-hundred-gallon sprayer truck for firefighting, which was stored near its barn. But use of this equipment meant calling company employees away from the orchards to operate the engine, dumping the oil used to control insects and replacing it with water before driving to the fire. The system was neither quick nor efficient, both important in firefighting. At the March 1950 meeting, the club agreed to match the donation of the Sweetwater Woman's Club of $25 toward the fire department, and club members were involved in a horse show in June 1950 that raised money for the fire department. The show netted enough money to buy a surplus California Department of Forestry engine, a 1931 Moreland. By August 1950, the Men's Club members were anticipating distributing business cards with the correct phone number for calling in a fire. In February 1951 the Sweetwater Men's Club hosted the First Annual Fireman's Ball on the one-year anniversary of the department's founding. The event netted nearly $500, at which time the new fire chief, Scofield Bonnet, told the attendees about the ten fires that the department had fought.

Working solely on donations, the volunteer fire department was underfunded, and it was eventually decided that the fire district should be funded through taxes. In addition to voting to endorse a "yes" vote for the fire district, while the issue was waiting for voter approval, the Men's Club solicited donations to keep the district funded. In January 1953, the local residents voted to create the Bonita-Sunnyside Fire Protection District by 140 to 4.

In 1951, in the minutes of the meeting from March, we find the first mention of incorporation of Bonita to forestall annexation by another neighbor city. It is the first, but not the last, mention of annexation and/or incorporation in a Men's Club meeting minutes. The minutes also record that the club regularly made donations to local causes, as its treasury would allow, especially events for children like the Sunnyside Friends Church's Halloween and Christmas parties.

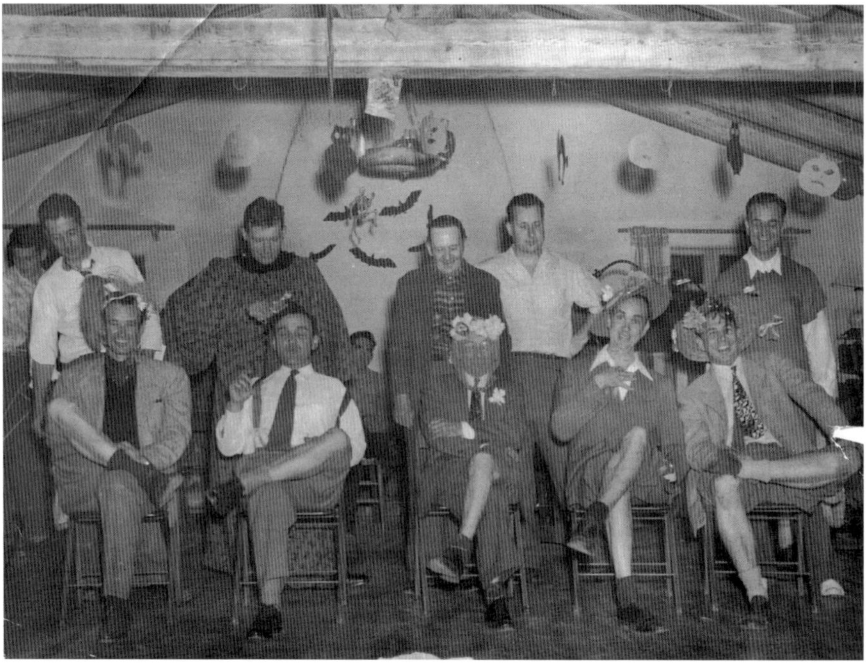

It was Halloween (probably 1955), and we know they were having a good time. *Front, left to right*: Bob Johnson, unknown, Michael Haubert, Steve Gassaway and Dick Wilson; *rear*: Bud Dring, Ham Marston, George Reynolds, Elmer Zinn and Jerry Oliver. *Bonita Museum & Cultural Center.*

Regular meetings continued to have a variety of speakers, including a representative of a local poultry association speaking about cooperative ventures, an expert on China, another expert on the future of defense production and a representative from the Southwest Highway Association about the importance of local roads to commerce. The club also held joint meetings with the Chula Vista Rotary and the Sweetwater Valley Civic Association. Some programs involved members offering slide and movie presentations of their travels.

Throughout the 1950s, the club continued to concern itself with safety issues of roads and signage in the valley. The group hosted speakers about the Nike guided missile and continuing civil defense issues. The Sweetwater Valley Civic Association facilitated discussion on the development in the valley, and members heard from a speaker on the pros and cons of forming a sewer district, an issue strongly related to local annexations.

In 1956, the men spent quite some time trying to create a recreation space behind the firehouse for the local kids. The land was leveled, and they had hopes of installing a volleyball net and basketball hoops to offer more activities for teenagers in the valley. It is out of this discussion that Secretary John Scudder wrote what the club members undertook as their philosophy (though the minutes make it hard to tell if there was an actual vote):

> *The traditional attitude of the Sweetwater Men's Club: we are interested in darn near everything—especially the welfare and happiness of this Valley and its people—we will look, listen, examine, investigate, admire, approve, reject, view with alarm, endorse, discuss and donate—but the only thing we will permit ourselves to follow through on seriously and consistently is to meet one a month and have dinner with our neighbors.*

It's quite an apt description. There's no record of what finally happened to the recreation area project.

Though spoken of only sparingly in the minutes, it does appear that after all the formal business was done, club members did partake of cards. Club meetings tended to wrap up by 10:00 p.m., though card games may have kept members until midnight or later. On a weeknight, no less. The one secretary who mentioned the games regularly commented that "those who won went away happy, and those who lost, did not."

By the mid-1960s, club membership was shrinking. It's not well understood through the documentation that presently exists why the club stopped operating or exactly when, but with the outside world not as far away from Bonita as it was in 1938, it's clear that the function the club served for the local residents was filled by other things. If in its nearly thirty years of operation the Sweetwater Men's Club achieved nothing other than helping found the Bonita Sunnyside Fire Protection District, that would be enough for it to be remembered. But for all the good it did both in the community and for the men who enjoyed its camaraderie, we should remember the club more fondly.

9

BROOKSIDE WINERY

Why Is There a Mission Building in Bonita?

So why is there a mission building in Bonita? During the time that Southern California was part of Spain, the Sweetwater Valley was part of El Rancho del Rey, the King's Ranch. During those years, it was primarily used for grazing cattle, and the profits from the cattle were used to support the soldiers who guarded the Presidio in San Diego. When the Spanish friars arrived in San Diego, there was a Native American settlement in the Sweetwater Valley that they called Apusquel. The names of some of the residents at that settlement were recorded in the registry books of the Mission San Diego, but no structure was ever built by the friars in the valley. An adobe structure was built as a residence for the caretaker of the ranch, and it was located somewhere near the structure we call Rohr Manor. So, no mission was built by the friars.

So, why does Bonita have a building that looks like a mission? Today, we take for granted that drinking wine at dinner is common, but in the years after World War II that was not true. Prohibition had decimated the ranks of winemakers in the United States, and Americans hadn't yet regrown a taste for drinking wine. Though Los Angeles is known as a region for growing citrus, the region was actually one of the premier grape growing regions in the United States in the 1890s, especially in Cucamonga in San Bernardino County. In the wake of Prohibition, however, many acres of grapes were removed, and few of the winemakers survived. The vineyards that did survive did so by offering sacramental wine and "grape tonic" or by replacing their wine vineyards with table grapes. A provision in the Volstead Act allowed for private ownership and consumption of wine, so many growers in Cucamonga continued to grow grapes that were sold for home winemaking, though they shifted to varietals that could better stand being transported around the country. Home winemaking during Prohibition grew from four million gallons to ninety million gallons in 1925.

One of the few winemakers who survived was Philo Biane, who was a third-generation winemaker operating out of Riverside. Philo's family established a winery in San Bernardino in 1882. A year later, they moved to Redlands Junction, and it was there that they started the first Brookside Winery. The four hundred acres they bought in San Timoteo Canyon ran alongside the creek that gave Brookside its name. Philo was born at the winery in 1909. As a child, he worked in the vineyards, and he later studied chemistry at St. Mary's College near Oakland. Because Prohibition was still in force when he graduated, he left the United States and studied winemaking in Europe. During World War II, he managed a food plant in San Francisco. Biane's family sold their winery late in the Prohibition years, but just before the war, they bought four hundred acres in Ontario. In 1952, they brought back the Brookside name, purchasing a plant built in 1904 from the California Wine Association. Philo returned to the family winery to help them expand their retail marketing.

Prohibition had changed American's taste in wine from dry wines served with food to sweet highly fortified wines as well as cheap jug wines that were affordable during the Depression. Indulging on something like wine during the war years was an uncommon thing, and it took several years after the war for the public to turn toward splurges like wine. Philo believed that the only way to get Americans back to drinking wine was to give them the opportunity to taste it before they bought it. To do that, he decided to capitalize on a small surge of public interest in wine and food tasting rooms all over California. Traditionally, the tasting room is a small space at the vineyard to allow interaction with the public, including wine tasting and sales. Philo believed that bringing the tasting room experience to where the public was would get them interested in wine. The first Brookside Winery Cellar tasting room was opened in 1954, and its success led to the building of more. In 1965, Brookside chose Bonita for the location of its seventh tasting room because of the region's growth.

The winery engaged the services of Victor Wulff, a local architect, and asked him to design a building appropriate for the location. The first vineyards in California had been planted by Junipero Serra at the

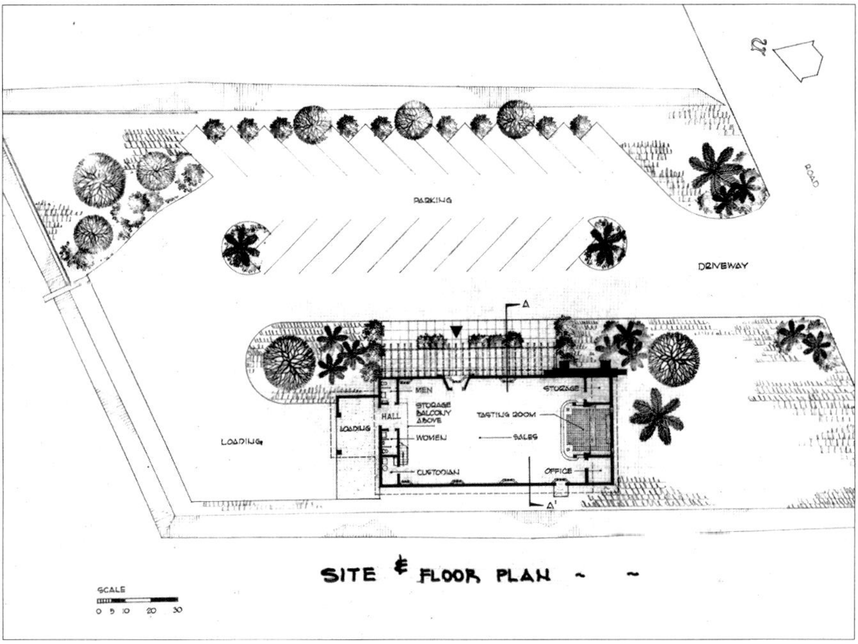

Victor Wulff's site plan for the Brookside Winery project. *Bonita Museum & Cultural Center.*

site of the San Diego Mission. The Biane family wanted the design for their sites to reflect this heritage. Wulff later stated that the Bianes' "love for the history of this western area, the mission fathers, the mission orchards and their vineyards—all play [*sic*] important roles in their modern grape culture, processing, and retailing." So, he was tasked with creating a building that encompassed historical heritage yet fulfilled the requirements of the business. It had to include a large sales room, a tasting bar, a small office, storage, public restrooms with a custodial space, a loading dock and parking. He referred to his design as "a structure which dared to be reminiscent of early California and yet modern in facility."

Victor Wulff had come to San Diego in 1941 after receiving both an undergraduate and graduate degree in architecture from Kansas University. After serving in the Navy during World War II, he joined the firm of William Templeton Johnston as a drafter and, after passing his exams, was offered a partnership. He had served on the Chula Vista Planning Commission and was appointed to a position on the Chula Vista City Council. He previously designed numerous buildings in the

South Bay, including several cottages at Frederica Manor, the Chula Vista Recreation Center, the Chula Vista Methodist Church and numerous banks and other business buildings.

Victor Wulff traveled, took photographs and investigated buildings like the one he was trying to mimic. After his research, he settled on a large space reminiscent of a refectory that would accommodate both gatherings as well as sales. The interior had heavy trussed beams and hand-textured and tinted plaster walls. The walls were built thick to look like they were made from adobe bricks, with deeply recessed windows to continue the illusion. The tiles on the roof were of varying exposures and were randomly placed so as to look aged even right after the building was completed. All of the exterior parts of the building, including the bell tower, were proportioned and designed to the size of the building. The exterior stucco was brushed with both brown and ivory paints to give a weathered effect to the building. The bell tower purposely had no bells because Wulff had determined that many historic missions could not afford them, and even when they did, they would often send those bells to other new missions, leaving their towers empty. A pergola running along the eastern side of the building was planted with grapevines to offer shade in the midday sun. That so many people thought the building dated from the mission era is clearly an homage to the talent of the architect and the craftsmen who built the building.

When the Brookside Winery Cellar No. 7 opened in Bonita in July 1965, it quickly became a beloved meeting place as well as a party venue. It was the site of many anniversary and birthday parties and even a fundraiser to buy bells for the empty bell tower of Lady of Guadalupe Church in Otay. It gave the valley a second meeting spot after the Sunnyside Steak Ranch. It was at the Brookside Winery that the Bonita Business and Professional Association hatched the idea of Bonitafest. And it was to the Brookside Winery that the organizers and VIPs of every Bonitafest retired at the end of each event to have a repast of wine, cheese and crackers.

At its height, the Brookside Winery operated thirty-four outlets in California as well as Arizona, Nevada and Illinois. It reproduced the Wulff mission design no fewer than eight times, including in such places as Tucson, Arizona, and Dundee, Illinois. In 1968, the family purchased Mills Winery in Sacramento, which included eleven retail sales and the tasting rooms. They eventually pared down those down to seven, three cellars in Sacramento and four more in the greater Bay Area. Through this acquisition, they obtained facilities and space to age more than three

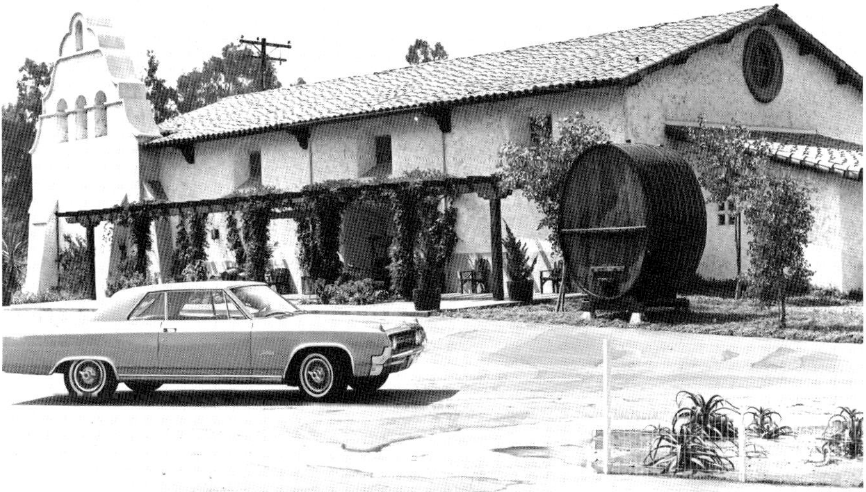

The front of the completed Brookside Tasting Room, 1965. *Bonita Museum & Cultural Center.*

and a half million gallons of wine. In addition to Bonita, Brookside had tasting rooms in El Cajon, Escondido and Pacific Beach. Also in 1968, Brookside bought 550 acres of property in the Temecula region to plant vines for wine, one of the first companies to see the potential for growing wine in that region.

Brookside sold its wines exclusively from its cellars, and people came to trust the wine they had tried in the tasting room. Some of the wines were sweeter, but many of them were what would be referred to as table wines, easy-drinking wines sold without a vintage year at affordable prices. The Brookside Cellars hosted countless events over the years for PTAs, service organizations, women's clubs, bridge clubs and just about anyone else who was interested in having an event with wine and cheese. It even used to buy back half-gallon and gallon bottles.

In 1973, Brookside merged with Beatrice Foods of Chicago. Brookside continued to act as a subsidiary of the larger company and continued to grow the wine business. The decision to merge was driven, in part, from a desire to grow into wholesale distribution, and the needed financial backing to do so. No money was paid; the deal was totally done by swapping stock in

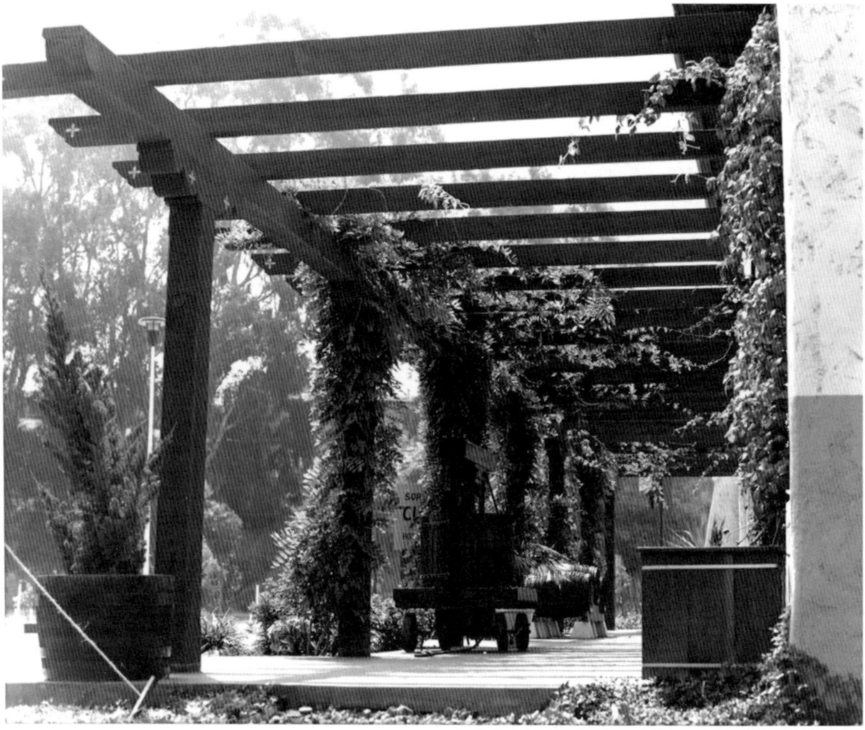

The pergola with its grapevines and the small details throughout the building were part of Victor Wulff's plan for the building to look timeworn. *Bonita Museum & Cultural Center.*

the companies. The Biane family continued to oversee everyday production and operations, and their headquarters remained at the Vineyard in Guasti. Philo left the business in 1974 and contented himself with tending the eighteen acres of grapes that surrounded his house, from which he made Triple Cream Sherry.

At one time, Brookside had over thirty outlets in four states, farmed three thousand acres of wine grapes and employed over three hundred people. It had also sold excess grapes to the Gallo Winery at a small profit as well as wine that had been fermented and fortified. At one time, Brookside shipped eight railcars of liquid every eight hours to Gallo. The merger with Brookside was a new venture for Beatrice Foods, and for a few years, the relationship worked well for both enterprises. But the smaller Brookside company often felt pushed around by Beatrice and didn't feel it was getting the financial backing it had been seeking when the deal was created.

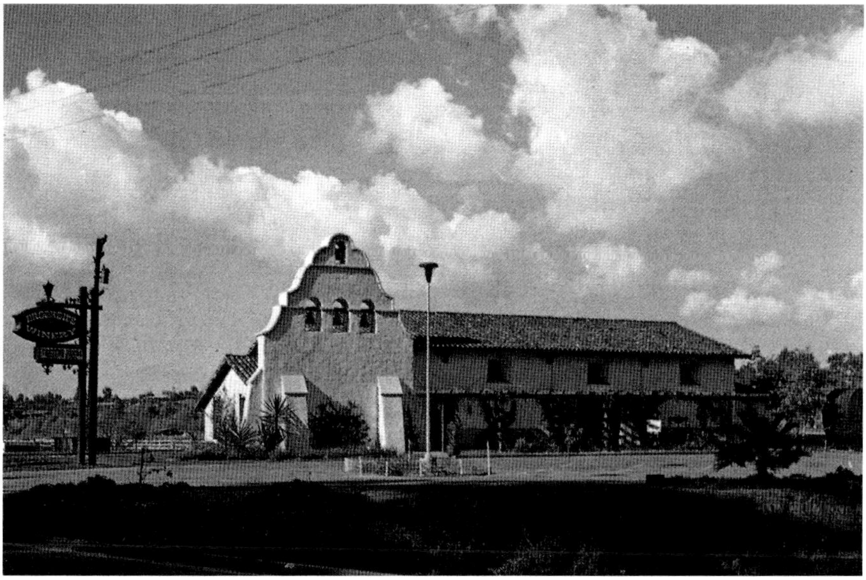

Postcard of the Brookside Winery Tasting Room No. 7. *Bonita Museum & Cultural Center.*

In 1982, some investors from San Francisco made Beatrice an offer she could not refuse, and Beatrice sold Brookside to them. The new owners saw Brookside's assets in terms of real estate, not winemaking, especially with the value of land in Southern California. A glut of wine grapes on the market in the early 1980s made Brookside seem an even less likely investment, and the new owners continued making wine only because they had grapes they couldn't otherwise get rid of.

Almost overnight, the new owners shuttered all but five of the tasting rooms. The remaining stores were rebranded as discount wine cellars, though they didn't continue to offer tasting. In April 1984, they auctioned off to the general public fixtures and vintage items that had been gathered from the closed tasting rooms. The remaining vineyards in Temecula as well as the Ontario bottling plant were both sold.

In May 1985, the remaining assets of Brookside Winery were sold at auction, including bottling equipment, storage tanks, bottling lines, refrigeration equipment and forklifts. The auction also included eighteen thousand board feet of redwood planks and 1,500 oak wine barrels. Philo Biane was philosophical, however: "You can't stop changing times. We've seen the wine business move around the state before. It moved here for a while, and now it has moved away." Two locations remained open, one at the original winery and another in Colton until July 1986, when all of the remaining wine was sold for pennies on the dollar.

Les and Marion Downs had worked at the Bonita winery since 1964, taking over the hosting job in 1968. They were given no warning and had no time to say goodbye to any of their customers, as all the remaining stock was returned to the vineyard. Locals' only option to buy Brookside wines was to drive to the remaining stores in the Los Angeles area and buy what they could get.

The new owners quickly worked to sell off the existing storefronts, including all of the various Victor Wulff–designed mission-inspired buildings. In 1982, they sold the Bonita location to the North Island Federal Credit Union. North Island had opened its original office in a strip mall in Bonita. The company modified the interior of the building to suit its purposes but retained the exterior architectural details and fixtures. The credit union remained in the building for twelve years before moving to an even larger building outside of Bonita. Chula Vista Cycle Sports, which opened on Central Avenue in Bonita in 1979 before moving to Telegraph Canyon Road in Chula Vista, bought the building to add another location. The interim owner had considered tearing down the building, but the Carrolls were able to buy it before that happened. Tom and Nadine Carroll gave this location the name Mission Cyclery in honor of the building. A few years later, their son Donny returned from professional bike racing in France, where he had learned to love the coffee. A few months later, Donny opened up a coffee cart on the walkway in the front of Mission Cyclery. Donny ran the cart in front of the bike shop for nine years before a renovation brought the coffee café inside. The Carrolls sold their stores to Performance Bike in 2003, but Donny's Café remains in the mission-inspired building to this day. It's still a place to meet a friend for a good drink, just coffee rather than wine.

Over the years, the other Victor Wulff–designed buildings have hosted offices, restaurants, retail stores, schools and, in one case, a church, not inappropriately. Most of the mission buildings were built to the same specifications as the store in Bonita, but a couple were actually shrunk down in size by a third to fit on smaller plots of land. Victor Wulff continued to work as an architect in the South Bay. He designed over twenty local elementary schools, including Valley Vista, which opened in the Sweetwater Valley in 1971. He also designed the Bonita Suites office building. He died in 1978 and left quite an architectural legacy in the South Bay.

An addendum to the Brookside winery story is that Philo's daughter still continues to make his Triple Cream Sherry under the name Rancho de Philo Winery, and in 2011, another Biane family descendant, Tim Bacino, restarted the Brookside Winery brand and is now bottling wines under that label in San Diego County. Drinking wine with meals is part of everyday life in the United States, so maybe Philo Biane was right all along.

10

WHY BONITA ISN'T A CITY

The Trials and Tribulations of Annexation and Incorporation

Prior to 1950, the Sweetwater Valley was sparsely populated, and there wasn't any reason to incorporate into a town. Zoning laws for the land were overseen by San Diego County government. The area had two stores and post offices, two schools, a gas station, a blacksmith and a church, as well as the businesses that were part of the citrus industry. Law enforcement was overseen by the sheriff's department, and fire services were part of the forestry division. Access to the valley was improved by the paving of Bonita and Sweetwater Roads completed in the 1930s. Travel to Chula Vista and National City was improved, making those cities' shopping districts readily available to valley residents. The Sweetwater Valley was a quiet little place, and that was the way everybody liked it.

Historically, citizens push to incorporate when they feel the need to provide a better service than the local county is offering. Citizens in the western United States often felt the need to incorporate to improve their water services, create laws against drinking or gambling or promote local trade or industries. Many cities that incorporated in the 1950s and 1960s did so to protect themselves from annexation by their neighbor cities. Opposition to incorporation is often based on a concern that taxes would increase or that the tax base won't be sufficient to support a city and the town will go bankrupt. Prior to the 1950s, none of these situations had existed in the Sweetwater Valley.

The first major change to the valley came just before World War II. The population of the valley had remained below five hundred through 1930 but had risen to nearly one thousand in 1940. The old wooden bridge that forded the Sweetwater River at Bonita was increasingly not up to the traffic it was carrying. In 1940, the county put out bids to build a concrete bridge across the Sweetwater River in Bonita. When construction of the bridge was completed, the realignment of the new bridge a few feet to the west allowed a curve in the approach on Sweetwater Road to be removed, making the road much safer. The new bridge was a welcome upgrade and would likely have been followed by others had not the war interrupted. In fact, in 1946, a similar bridge was built on the east end of the valley in Sunnyside.

In the years just after the war, the San Diego County Planning Commission began to look again at zoning for the Sweetwater Valley. The first two meetings were held in August 1946, and local input was achieved through a commission of three local citizens who polled residents by visiting their homes for their opinions. Both the boundaries and the various zoning types were haggled over, but nothing concrete came out of those early meetings.

In 1949, San Diego County Planning Commission again tried again to change some zoning in the valley, and there was some opposition, much of it very concerned with "what's in it for us." In October 1949, a new zoning plan of the valley, created by the county planning commission, was finally approved by San Diego County. The plan set up business areas at the intersection of the Bonita and Willow Roads and farther west on National and Highland Avenues and zoned the rest of the valley up to the present-day Otay Lakes Road for agriculture and half- to one-acre residential parcels. Opposition to the plan was stated as loss of control of the rights of one's property, the leading group against the changes being known as the Constitutional Rights Protective Association.

Also in 1949, an influential group of local citizens banded together to form the Sweetwater Valley Civic Association (SVCA) with the purpose of maintaining a rural atmosphere in the valley. Though not all participants in the fight over the planning commission's plan became members of the Sweetwater Valley Civic Association, it's clear that the fight over this plan motivated many locals to create an organization that would give them a stronger voice in such decisions. Though some of the initial members were from the "first families" of the valley, the general membership was dominated by residents who had been attracted to the valley subsequent to World War II because of its relative isolation. In the years following the war, this group would be at the forefront of protecting the valley.

The initial motivation for organizing the SVCA was action against the California Division of Highway's proposal to acquire the right-of-way and construct State Highway 54 through the valley, closely following the present alignment of Bonita Road. Because of their intervention, a feasibility study was conducted and the results submitted to the San Diego County Board of Supervisors, which led to the cancellation of the plans for the highway. In the months after the successful fight against the highway, the SVCA suffered some infighting, which led it to go dormant for several years.

Back in 1946, some former orchard acreage had been divided into lots for home construction. These early postwar subdivisions only involved selling plots of land to other owners for them to build, but they did usher in an era of more rapid growth and development. Some tracts were as small as 5 one-acre building sites, though others were as large as 47 sites. All remained half an acre or larger parcels, and all required septic systems. Altogether, by 1950, over 180 parcels of land had been offered for sale in the valley. As much as the local residents wanted to protect the rural nature of the Sweetwater Valley, the sale of previously agricultural land in the Sweetwater Valley was encouraging the growth of population dramatically, leading to the building of more retail establishments as well as the addition of an elementary school and the creation of a fire district. Having the appropriate infrastructure for the residents was starting to be an issue.

In 1959, a proposal was made for a sand- and gravel-processing plant and rock-crushing operation on the east side of the Sunnyside Bridge as well as a reopening of the rock quarry located near the dam. This plan brought residents out in droves to oppose it, and their opposition to the planning commission's recommendation in favor of the permit forced the county supervisors to hold a hearing. The commissioners voted 3–2 against the permit. This local fight brought about interest in renewing the Sweetwater Valley Civic Association, which happened in December 1959. In the new structure, a member represented each of nine districts within the Valley, forming a board, with general membership for any resident of the valley. (The board eventually grew to twenty-two.) The association's first official action was to state its opposition to the sand and gravel pit, though the vote had already been made against it. Within two years, the SVCA went on record against another sand and gravel operation in the valley.

The power of the SVCA and local opposition led some landowners who were unable to obtain the desired zoning from the county government to turn to either Chula Vista or National City, where the owner could make prezoning a condition of the annexation. Once the annexation was complete, the owner could continue with development on their terms. As a means of circumventing SVCA influence, National City annexed 18.74 acres of land in 1959, and in 1960, Chula Vista annexed two parcels totaling 98.20 acres. These annexations, on the floodplain near Highland Avenue, brought the city boundaries of Chula Vista and National City together. In each case, the parcels, located at the mouth of the valley near the Sweetwater River, were rezoned for commercial or industrial use.

These shots over the bow of the valley's health led the SVCA Board to seriously consider the prospect of incorporation. The minutes of the SVCA meeting on July, 26, 1960, record that a motion was "Moved, Seconded and passed that directors have a study made of the feasibility of incorporating the valley." The Public Affairs Research Institute of San Diego State College was commissioned to conduct the feasibility study for incorporation, and the report was submitted on November 22, 1960. Based on the Lakewood Plan, the report found that incorporation was feasible to preserve existing land use pattern and retain existing levels of public services. The contents of the report were favorable, and circulated petitions in the spring of 1961 called for an election on the subject of incorporation.

Once petitions were delivered, the County Board of Supervisors was required to call a hearing to determine whether 51 percent or more of the land owners' assessed value (based on the county assessor's valuation of land) was against incorporation. If that level was achieved, then the petitions were denied and the attempt at incorporation would fail. At the meeting, the supervisors based their decision to end the matter on the word of the county assessor's office that 56 percent of owners were against incorporation. Those in favor of incorporation found a discrepancy and asked for a recount, which the board of supervisors asked the assessor to do.

Since the law under which this attempt at incorporation was happening was relatively new, there was no precedent, and the county board of supervisors decided that it needed a court's decision to proceed. The supervisors then asked the people of Bonita who were in favor of incorporation to sue them. Once the case reached a hearing, the judge determined that even though the board of supervisors had been in error in its decision to close the attempted incorporation, it was under no obligation to reopen the matter. This particular attempt at incorporation was done, and no new attempt at incorporation could be started until a calendar year after the meeting was held. In lieu of actually incorporating, the Sweetwater Valley Civic Association took a vote in determination to retain the rural atmosphere in the valley, though it was only binding on the organization itself. But outside interest in annexations of properties inside the valley continued apace.

Feeling that incorporation was at least temporarily a dead end, the SVCA continued to look to ways to protect the valley. The first attempt, in January 1962, was to propose annexing all of the Bonita-Sunnyside Fire Protection District to the City of Chula Vista, allowing any sub district to remove itself from the annexation if they so desired. The association hoped that by creating pre-zoning of this package annexation it would protect the rural nature of the valley. There was some opposition, but the proposal died in part because of lack of interest from the City of Chula Vista. The association realized that the loss of a package deal meant that piecemeal annexations would continue, and it would have to continue to fight indefinitely.

In August 1962, eight and a half acres of land along Otay Lakes Road that had previously been annexed was rezoned commercial despite the protests of adjacent landowners, the Bonita Village Shopping Center and even the staff of the planning department. In September, Gordon Pettit and Dick Williams, the primary movers behind Bonita Village Shopping Center, proposed annexing the village and other property they owned, totaling one hundred acres, to the City of Chula Vista in part for assistance with sewer service. The SVCA voted to be neutral on the village annexation. Though the boundaries were adjusted somewhat over the next few weeks, in December 1962, ninety-seven acres in the heart of Bonita were annexed to Chula Vista. This included both sides of Bonita Road from the Bonita Bridge to Otay Lakes Road—not including the golf course fairways—as well as land adjoining the north side of the Sweetwater River. This annexation included the fire station for the Bonita Sunnyside Fire Protection District, necessitating an agreement between that agency and the Chula Vista City Fire Department as to which would protect the annexed portion of the valley and how it would be paid for. In addition, another dozen or so smaller annexations were completed to Chula Vista and National City by the end of the year.

So, here's a little bit of an excursion into the background of growth in California in the years after World War II. The population explosion after the war caused problems for municipalities in California. Special districts were being created by developers to supply urban services such as water, roads, fire protection and sewers, which gave local municipalities responsibility for these services without the commensurate tax base to go with it. In addition, cities had begun to annex property somewhat willy-nilly as a way to increase their tax basis, and that led to even more fragmentary annexations. The State of California tried to create a state commission to oversee these boundary issues, but the commission found that it was too far removed from the local concerns to be able to deal effectively with complex local issues. In 1963, the California legislature passed a bill that created commissions in each county that would oversee proposed annexations and special districts. A Local Agency Formation Commission (hereafter LAFCO) was created in each county to scrutinize the ideas behind special districts and annexations to create a harmonized community. LAFCO in San Diego was going to play a large part in why Bonita remained unincorporated.

Also, in 1963, Bonita engaged in a fight to retain its own post office. Word came down that postal officials wanted to consolidate the Bonita office into a satellite post office of Chula Vista. Their arguments were that mail service would be delivered faster and that all of the valley would be covered by the same post office. (At the time, mail service to the valley was divided between the Chula Vista, National City, Bonita and Sunnyside Post Offices.) It took several months and the involvement of the local congressmen, but in 1964, the merger was off and Bonita retained not only its own post office but its own postal imprint as well.

The gradual, haphazard annexations continued apace. Chula Vista annexed over 700 acres in twenty separate annexations and National City over 550 acres in twenty-three parcels. The largest acquisitions included the two golf courses—in 1966 Chula Vista purchased Rohr Park from the Rohr Aircraft Employees Association and annexed the park along with the golf course, and in 1970, the owner of the Bonita Golf Course applied for and was granted the right to annex to National City. The National City parcel was immediately rezoned to accommodate a major commercial shopping center. The Bonita Golf Course continued operations pending development for nearly ten years, including a case that went all the way to the California Supreme Court. Complaints to the county about neighbors keeping farm animals, like horses and chickens, continued to rise though they remained the exception not the rule.

Prior to 1963, the controlling agency in determining lot sizes in the valley was the San Diego County Public Health Department, since no sewer facilities existed prior to that year. In 1963, however, a Metropolitan Sewer District trunk line was completed, and for the first time, large-scale subdivision activity was possible. In 1964, the first annexation under the control of LAFCO took place as Chula Vista annexed a portion of property near Allen School and Bonita Roads. From that time through 1968, subdivision activity was very low in the valley, possibly because of the new regulations required by appearing before LAFCO. In 1965, both National City and Chula Vista created master plans that included overlapping portions of the Sweetwater

Valley becoming part of their cities, a development that left valley residents concerned about being gobbled up whole with no say in the matter. Both city management teams seemed to believe that the local residents would annex to whichever city gave them the "best package."

In May 1968, Corky McMillin was able to have 113.5 acres of land in the valley rezoned by the County Planning Commission to R1 (10,000 square feet per lot) and R1(15) (hilly sites, half acre per lot). Over the years, six separate subdivision maps were recorded for this property, which brought the first large-scale development to the valley. Nearly four houses could be built on every acre, rather than the one or two that had previously been allowed. And the McMillin Company built an oversized trunk line for the connection to the sewer, one would that ultimately allow for nearly 1,000 homes, far greater than the 230 homes that were initially announced. Later in the year, the LAFCO commissioners voted to approve the annexation of those properties to the Spring Valley Sanitation District, the first of many such annexations LAFCO allowed in the valley.

In the fall of 1968, the Chula Vista City Council approved the Chula Vista Planning Commission's request to form a committee of Sweetwater Valley residents to work on a pre-zoning plan for the valley. The Sweetwater Valley Planning Committee, made up of fifteen local residents and property owners, was introduced in January 1969. A single plan that could guide future annexations in an orderly fashion, using input from local residents, was considered the best hope for preserving the valley, especially by Chula Vista. Some locals thought this was a good idea, but others (especially those living in Sunnyside) thought it just a prequel for Chula Vista's total annexation of the valley. The Chula Vista City Council tabled the idea for six months in October 1969, and in May 1970, council members forwarded all of their work to the county rather than continue to go forward. Chula Vista continued to complain that the LAFCO commissioners were approving the expansion of special districts, even against the recommendations of its own staff, but not encouraging annexations to cities, which was ostensibly the reason for the law, leading to unwieldy boundaries and lost tax dollars.

In August 1970, the mayor of Chula Vista, deciding to take the bull by the horns, sent a letter to all valley residents stating the desire of Chula Vista to annex the entire rural portion of the valley. Previously content to sit on the sidelines, Chula Vista decided to act decisively. Mayor Tom Hamilton believed that the best hope of preserving the valley and its rural character lay in annexation, and he was ready to go forward, taking the entire valley rather than small pieces. "Chula Vista is ready to make a commitment, and the valley residents must make their commitment," said the mayor, making his offer sound an awful lot like a wedding proposal. Chula Vista was prepared to create a "Valley Zone" that would be different than other existing zoning areas of Chula Vista, determined to protect the rural nature of the valley. The Sweetwater Valley Civic Association's initial vote was to remain neutral on the annexation move (though many members were in favor of annexation). Some local horse owners came out in favor of the zoning that Chula Vista was proposing, finding it superior to the county's existing zoning.

The opposition, the Valley Planning Association (VPA), had formed in November 1970 to explore incorporation and included many of the owners of undeveloped parcels of land and those involved in real estate sales. Its stated goal was to obtain information regarding both the advantages and disadvantages of incorporation, and objections were based on concerns that zoning regulations imposed by Chula Vista would be more stringent that those of San Diego County. In February 1971, the VPA released a report that it had commissioned on the possible solutions. It listed incorporation as possible but unfeasible because of lack of business revenue within the boundaries and that annexation to another city would result in virtually no voice in the politics of the area. Since the report made no judgment of which course of action to take, residents took what they liked and disregarded the rest.

Owners of one-half to one-acre lots with horses and corrals expressed concerns that they would lose the right to keep horses on their property, even as Chula Vista officials assured them that would not be the case. (A survey by the Bonita Valley Horsemen listed 980 horses in the valley in 1971, about 1 horse for every two people.) Fear over annexation often turned to fear of being citified, including the need for sidewalks, curbs and gutters and strict control of farm-type animals. Proponents of annexation were accused of selling neighbors down the river, and opponents were called greedy land developers. Neighbors' relationships were profoundly tested in many parts of the valley.

After some investigation, the prevailing best plan, according to the SVCA, was annexation through what was called the Bellevue Plan. Based on annexations to Bellevue, Washington, the areas annexed would retain a community council that wielded power over development, zoning, animal regulations and other land use issues. (Other options the SVCA listed were—stay under county government, form a county service area under the county, incorporate as a separate city or annex to Chula Vista with no special considerations.) If the Bellevue Plan was adopted, it would offer the local residents nearly the same power over their destinies as residents of Chula Vista. The leading proponent of the Bellevue Plan was Pat Spies, a resident and an original member of the SCVA. There were differences in the way the plan would play out in California, but Mayor Hamilton was of the opinion that the community councils were not necessary because annexed land could be pre-zoned, which was not allowed in Washington. Local proponents of annexation said community control was essential.

A local professor at Southwestern College, Wilbur Switzer, had his students conduct a survey in the winter of 1970–71. They spoke to over 1,500 residents. (Switzer also lived in the valley.) Their survey, which was released in February 1971, showed 52 percent of the local residents "favoring the status quo as a means of keeping the valley's identity," with 88 percent indicating that the rural nature of the valley, or open space, was the key factor they identified with their community. Over 70 percent believed that any political change would endanger the identity of the valley. So, the prevailing opinion seemed to be do nothing and hope things worked out.

By the summer of 1971, the proponents of annexation had circulated petitions that enabled them to get the annexation issue placed on the ballot with a special election scheduled for October 1971, though there was a failed attempt by the VPA to obtain enough signatures to stop the election. In September, after a closed-door meeting that lasted well into the night, the Sweetwater Valley Civic Association voted to endorse a "yes" vote on annexation, with the inclusion of a pre-zoning plan, reasonable animal regulation and some form of community council as part of the deal. Some members of the SVCA, most notably Pat Spies, were the victims of harassing phone calls and threats of violence during this time, a very ugly side of this battle. (Pat Spies would retire from the SCVA in 1977 after thirty years of service to the community.)

After nearly a year of name-calling, heated arguments, threats both over the phone and by letter, even one fistfight, the measure finally came to the ballot on October 26, 1971. On Election Day, the measure failed by 1,379 votes against and 737 for, with 71 percent of the registered voters casting ballots. Whether the failure was an actual vote against annexation or just against a change to the status quo, the results were the same. The implications were felt the next day when the mayor of Chula Vista said, not unlike a jilted groom at the altar,

> *They* [the valley residents] *have said that we don't want your services and we don't want your planning. Historically Chula Vista has turned down requested annexations that don't conform to the character of the valley. But now we will have to look at these from a standpoint of whether they would be good development for Chula Vista and how they pertain to our zoning and city development.*

Though the piecemeal annexations of the valley had been on hold in the run up to the election, within three months of the vote, annexations were again going strong. By the end of 1972, a total of 1,215 residential dwellings were either under construction or had been approved, enough new residents to raise the valley population by nearly 50 percent. In the fall of 1972, the residents approved a county-sponsored citizens' planning committee for the valley.

Alongside the annexation and incorporation battle was a related change in local land use. As early as the 1960s, there were calls to create a county park around the Sweetwater River, but it wasn't until 1971 that the first plans were proposed for Sweetwater Valley Regional Park. The plan called for preservation of the flood-prone areas with construction of picnic areas, hiking and riding trails and a nature interpretive area. It also stated that the planners believed that creation of the park was the best hope for preserving open space in the Sweetwater Valley. Voices in opposition to the park, led by the VPA, feared an increase in their property values and taxes, added traffic on their roads and that the park would turn into a "hippie haven." Owners whose property stood in the floodplain were not happy about having to move and the compensation that the county was planning to offer for their land. Infighting over the VPA's position on the park was part of its eventual dissolution. It took a decade before the bulk of the land necessary for the park was purchased or condemned by San Diego County.

In the years after the vote, another inroad into the valley was opened. Interstate 805 provided an alternate route to Interstate 5 from the city of San Diego and the border. Named after Jacob Dekema, a pioneering force from Caltrans who helped shape the San Diego freeway system, I-805 was completed in the summer of 1975. Unlike Interstate 5, which crossed the far west of the Sweetwater River, 805 came through a portion of Bonita. In fact, the land that now lies to the west of the highway, considered Chula Vista, was previously considered part of Bonita. The opening of the highway and the later connection of East H Street with Otay Lakes Road opened up access to previously undeveloped land to the south and east of Bonita. At this same time, the horse population actually grew as a result of horses being pushed out of other local communities.

In 1981, the idea of annexation to Chula Vista returned. The SVCA commissioned a study by San Diego State University on the subject of annexation. The subcommittee was formed for four reasons:

> *1) Frustration with county board of supervisors on planning and monitoring of projects*
> *2) Recognition that more acres in the valley had been lost to Chula Vista in the decade since the vote*
> *3) Changes in a Chula Vista city ordinance that would allow for the formation of a community planning group for Bonita should annexation take place*
> *4) Issues with the accountability of local county officials to the Sweetwater Valley community*

One of the newer arguments in favor of annexation was that the number of people in the valley as a voting bloc in Chula Vista would be 14 percent of registered voters rather than a 1 percent position as part of San Diego County. In addition, the valley voted in an election for only two of the supervisors, and the remainder carried no loyalty to the region over their own districts. Chula Vista chose to remain neutral in this particular instance, fearing that any other position would provoke a negative response. The SVCA annexation committee's recommendation that the county do a feasibility study was voted down by the membership, and the issue faded into the background again.

In 1987, a few folks met and formed Citizens for a Better Bonita. Central to their effort at annexation to Chula Vista was that they would stop if they could not have guarantees of retention of the rural atmosphere of Bonita. The committee needed to reach 350 signatures before it could get LAFCO to consider the matter, and they wanted to get a definitive study from LAFCO as to what annexation would mean to the valley. LAFCO reported that it would require a pre-zoning of all 7.7 square miles of the land as well as a state-mandated environmental review before it would consider the proposal. The drive continued apace, and an election was scheduled, but opponents stopped it with a petition drive.

By the late 1980s, with the county planning group and other agencies looking out for the remaining open space in the valley, talk of annexation or incorporation had all but died. The residents who would fight to "keep the valley the way it is" had essentially won every battle, though in the larger war, the valley had lost hundreds of acres to annexations and development. By the mid-1980s, Chula Vista was busy with the Eastlake development and the eventual annexation of Otay Ranch, where the population would double from 8,400 in 1980 to 17,500 in 2000. Other than its success at annexing and building Plaza Bonita, National City was for the most part unable to access further land in the valley.

After nearly twenty years, two updates to the plan and a handful of lawsuits, the new Sweetwater Regional Park celebrated its opening in May 1992, including the Sweetwater Summit Campground with sixty spaces. The park also included facilities for horse camping, bringing visitors to the valley. From the campground, hiking and riding trails followed the Sweetwater River bed all the way to the bay or east to the top of San Miguel Mountain. The park had preserved a large amount of open space surrounding the Sweetwater River bed from the area of the dam to the 805 freeway.

Today, the Sweetwater Valley contains a lot of open space and continues to retain a far more rural character than many places in San Diego County. As Bruce Warren said in 1974, it is the "acres of open spaces surrounding the many areas of Bonita, that are the only thing that makes it rural." The horses do not outnumber people, but there are still trails and horses in the valley, as well as organizations like the Sunnyside Saddle Club and the Bonita Valley Horsemen. And after five attempts at either annexation or incorporation over fifty years, Bonita retains its rural nature, but it's still just unincorporated San Diego County land.

In 1940, the Sweetwater Valley consisted of about 7,500 acres of land with around 900 people living there, at a density of 1.1 person per acre. By 2010, the valley had 30 percent less acreage with 12,500 people living there at a density of nearly 4 people per acre. Some battles over development were won, but others (like the large-scale development of Bonita Highlands and Bonita Long Canyon) were lost. Large chunks of land, like the Bonita Golf Course, now the site of Plaza Bonita, were lost to National City. Chula Vista claimed the entire central business district of Bonita as long ago as the 1960s. If you could go back in a time machine to 1950-something and you knew what would be lost or gained fifty years on, what choice would you make?

BIBLIOGRAPHY

Primary sources for this book have been archives of the *San Diego Union*, *Evening Tribune*, *San Diego Sun*, *Chula Vista Star-News*, *National City Record*, *Los Angeles Times* and *Los Angeles Herald*, as well as personal interviews by the author with: Bob Basile, Giles Brown, Mike Campbell, John Crosse, Virginia Crumrine, Maryanne Savary, Beau Mitchum, Glenn and Jo Morrison, Vincent Rossi, Susan E. Schnare and Laurence Weisser Jr.

Allen, Ella Bradford, "A Trip to San Pedro Martyr Mountain" (unpublished manuscript, no date). Bonita Museum & Cultural Center Archives.

Allen, Mrs. R.C. *The History of Bonita.* Bonita, CA: Bonita Museum & Cultural Center Archives, 1934.

Beltran, David Jimenez. *The Agua Caliente Story: Remembering Mexico's Legendary Racetrack.* Lexington, KY: Eclipse Press, 2004.

Briggs, Lillian. Oral History Interview with Mary Ward, April 27, 1979. Transcript. SDHS Oral History Program, San Diego History Center, San Diego, California.

Browne, Patrick. "The Cashiering of Major Robert Morris Copeland." Historical Digression. August 14, 2015. https://historicaldigression.com/2015/08/14/the-cashiering-of-major-robert-morris-copeland.

Bryant, Keith L., Jr. *History of the Atchison, Topeka & Santa Fe Railway.* Lincoln: University of Nebraska Press, 1974.

California State Board of Horticulture. *Annual Report for 1892.* Sacramento, CA: Superintendent State Printing, 1892.

Canadian Great War Project. "Bombardier Henry Grafton Chapman." Accessed January 15, 2018. https://cgwp.uvic.ca/detail.php?pid=922484.

Carrico, Richard L., Susan H. Carrico, Kathleen A. Crawford and S. Katherine Flanigan. *Historic Resources Inventory: Sweetwater Valley*. Prepared for County of San Diego: Unknown binding, 1990.

Chula Vista Historical Society. *Chula Vista, the Early Years.* Vols. 1–7. San Diego, CA: Tecolote Publications, 1992–2000.

———. *Family, Friends, and Homes.* San Diego CA: Tecolote Publications, 1991.

Cohen, Hannah S., and Gloria G. Harris. *Remarkable Women of San Diego.* Charleston, SC: The History Press, 2016.

Coleman, Eugene Victor. "The Urbanization of the Sweetwater Valley." Master's thesis, San Diego State University, 1973.

Copeland, Frederick W. "The Righteous Major." *Atlantic* (March 1961): 69–74.

Copeland, R. Morris. *Country Life: A Handbook of Agriculture, Horticulture and Landscape Gardening.* Amherst: University of Massachusetts Press, 2009.

coxefamily. Tumblr post. http://coxefamily.tumblr.com

Crosse, John. "Frank Mead: 'A New Type of Architecture in the Southwest,' Part 1, 1890–1906." Southern California Architectural History. https://socalarchhistory.blogspot.com/2016/05/frank-mead-new-kind-of-architecture-in.html.

———. "Frank Mead: 'A New Type of Architecture in the Southwest,' Part 2, 1907–1920." Southern California Architectural History. https://socalarchhistory.blogspot.com/2016/05/frank-mead-new-type-of-architecture-in.html.

Decisions of the Railroad Commission of the State of California. Volume 8. California: State Printing Office, 1916.

Eddy, Lucinda, "Frank Mead and Richard Requa," in *Toward a Simpler Way of Life*. Berkeley, CA: Norfleet Press, 1997.

Eisen, Gustav. *The Raisin Industry: A Practical Treatise on the Raisin Grapes, Their History, Culture and Curing.* San Francisco, CA: H.S. Crocker & Company, 1890.

Esterbloom, Gloria L. *This, Our Beloved Valley.* National City, CA: South Bay Press, 1954.

Estes, Donald H. *South Bay Monogatari: Tales of the South Bay Nikkei Community (Chula Vista the Early Years).* San Diego, CA: Tecolote Publications, 1996.

Fetzer, Leland. *San Diego County Place Names A to Z.* San Diego, CA: Sunbelt Publications, 2005.

Guinn, J.M. *Historical and Biographical Record of Southern California*. Chicago: Chapman Publishing Company, 1902.

Harvard College. *25th Anniversary Report of the Secretary of the Class of 1881 of Harvard College*. Cambridge, MA: Riverside Press, 1906.

Hastings, Edgar F. Oral History with Morris Allen, March 17, 1960. SDHS Oral History Program, San Diego History Center, San Diego CA.

Howell, Loraine Price. *Sweetwater Woman's Club History 1911–1976*. Unknown Binding. Bonita Museum & Cultural Center Archives.

Howell, Loraine P., and Zelma Klicka. *History of the Sweetwater Woman's Club or "The Way We Were to the Way We Are" 1911–1995*. Unknown Binding. Bonita Museum & Cultural Center Archives.

Kneeland, Marilyn. "The Modern Boston Tea Party—The San Diego Suffrage Campaign of 1911." *Journal of San Diego History* (Fall 1977). https://www.sandiegohistory.org/journal/1977/october/suffrage.

La Force, J.C. "Appraisal of Sweetwater Fruit Company Property." Unpublished manuscript, San Diego History Center Archives.

Leiser, Edward L. "San Diego Flying Days." Books 1, 11 and 12. Unpublished manuscript, 1995. San Diego Air and Space Museum Archives.

Lowell, Douglas L. "The California Southern Railroad and the Growth of San Diego." *Journal of San Diego History*, Fall 1985. http://www.sandiegohistory.org/journal/1985/october/railroad-8.

McClain, Molly. "A Room of Their Own: The Contribution of Women to the Panama-California Exposition, 1915." *Journal of San Diego History* (Winter 2015). https://www.academia.edu/16439690/A_Room_of_Their_Own_The_Contribution_of_Women_to_the_Panama-California_Exposition_1915.

McGrew, Clarence Alan. *City of San Diego and San Diego County: The Birthplace of California*. Vol. 2. San Diego, CA: American Historical Society, 1922.

Menzel, Spencer L. "The Development of the Sweetwater Area (California)." Master's thesis, University of Southern California, 1942. http://sunnycv.com/steve/local/docs/doc228.pdf.

Munoz, Cynthia Munoz, and Cheryl Smith. Oral History with Mary Ward, date unknown. Bonita Museum & Cultural Center Archives.

National Soaring Museum. "William Hawley Bowlus." https://www.soaringmuseum.org/pdf/hof/pdf8_pdfbio.pdf.

Phillips, Irene. *The Chula Vista Story 1868–1968*. National City, CA: South Bay Press, 1968.

———. "National City in Review," *San Diego Historical Society Quarterly* (July 1962).

———. *National City, Pioneer Town.* National City, CA: South Bay Press, 1960.

——— *The Story of El Rancho de la Nación.* National City, CA: South Bay Press, 1959.

———. *The Story of El Rancho de la Nación—"Land & Town" Edition.* National City, CA: South Bay Press, 1959.

Saum, Lewis O. "The Proctor Interlude in St. Joseph and in America: Astronomy, Romance and Tragedy." *American Studies International* (February 1999):34–54. http://www.ianridpath.com/atlases/Proctor_in_America.PDF.

Schnare, Susan E. "The Exeter Landscape Designs of Robert Morris Copeland." *Historical New Hampshire* (Spring 2008): 19–40.

Schoenherr, Steven, Mary E. Oswell and the Bonita Museum & Cultural Center. *Bonita.* Charleston SC: Arcadia Publishing, 2009.

Seaver, Frederick, J. *Historical Sketches of Franklin County and its Several Town: With Many Short Biographies.* Albany, NY: J.B. Lyon Company, 1918.

Sherman, Frederick S. *The Ancestry of Samuel Sterling Sherman and Mary Ware Allen.* Oakland: California Genealogical Society & Library, 2017.

Smithsonian National Air and Space Museum. "Carl Myers Balloon Farm Collection 1889–1910." https://airandspace.si.edu/collection-objects/carl-myers-balloon-farm-collection-1889-1910.

Stigall, Gary. "Fires Disrupt San Diego Broadcasts." Society of Broadcast Engineers–San Diego. http://sbe36.org/2007/10/fires-disrupt-san-diego-broadcasts.

Tishler, William H. Introduction to the Reprint Edition of Robert Morris Copeland's "A Country Life." Library of American Landscape History. http://lalh.org/wp-content/uploads/2012/04/COPELAND_Intro.pdf.

Vanderwood, Paul J. *Stan's Playground: Mobsters and Movie Star at American's Greatest Gaming Resort.* Berkeley, CA: University Press Books, 2009

Van Wormer, Stephen R. "Alfred H. Isham: A Gilded Age Entrepreneur in San Diego County." *Southern California Quarterly* (Winter 1982): 303–33.

Walker, George M., and John Peragine. *Cucamonga Valley Wine.* Charleston SC: The History Press, 2017.

Weld, Christopher Minot. Christopher Minot Weld to Theodore Roosevelt. 1901. In the Roosevelt Center at Dickinson State University. http://www.theodorerooseveltcenter.org/Research/Digital-Library/Record.aspx?libID=o36418.

Wulff, Victor. "Brookside Winery." Unpublished manuscript. Bonita Museum & Cultural Center archives.

Yokley, Richard C. *Story of Fire Protection in the Sweetwater Valley.* Bonita, CA: Bonita Museum & Cultural Center, 1993.

Zivotsky, Ann. "KPBS Returns to Its Frequency." *San Diego Union-Tribune*, October 25, 2007. http://www.sandiegouniontribune.com/sdut-kpbs-returns-to-its-frequency-2007oct25-story.html.

INDEX

L

M

N

O

P

ABOUT THE AUTHOR

Mary E. Oswell is a native of Bonita who attended Ella B. Allen Elementary and Bonita Vista Junior High and has a bachelor of arts in anthropology. She remembers buying treats at the candy counter in the Bonita Store and riding the ponies at Bradley Stables. After a short stint in the real world after college, she took her background into the nonprofit sphere and worked at the Maritime Museum of San Diego and the San Diego Automotive Museum before being both a volunteer and employee of the Bonita Museum & Cultural Center. She was part of the capital campaign team that brought the Bonita Museum & Cultural Center to its new home in 2006, and in 2009, she coauthored Images of America: *Bonita* with Dr. Steven Schoenherr. In 2011, she left San Diego to move to Colorado, where she continues to volunteer at local history museums and collect stories of local history.